OUR LITTLE CROATIAN CORNER

A Personal Memoir

by

Ana Bosiljevac Jarmek

Our Little Croatian Corner

Copyright © 2011 by Ana Bosiljevac Jarmek

ISBN: 978-0-9849217-0-6

Published by *AlphaGraphics 190*

Dedication

To my husband, Ivan,

to our children, Brian and Simone,

and to the joys of my life –

our two grandchildren, Amanda and Joshua.

Acknowledgments

Thanks to my father, who updated me with all of the family history information as well as the history of the community where we were born. He also taught me to understand the political atmosphere of our time, as well as important events in Croatian history.

Thanks to my mother, who got me interested in reading, although neither she nor I had the opportunity for higher education.

Special thanks to my new friend Julia Johnson, who enabled me to complete this memoir that I had written over a ten-year period. She fixed my problems with spelling and grammar and edited my work by figuring out what I wanted to say.

My appreciation to my friend Millie Sambol, who found the right editor for me, and supplied for this book some rare photographs of her relatives in Grice and of items from her family's museum.

FORWARD

I am part of the sun as my eye is part of me. That I am part of the earth my feet know perfectly, and my blood is part of the sea. My soul knows that I am part of the human race...as my spirit is part of my nation. In my own very self, I am part of my family.

D. H. Lawrence, **Apocalypse** *[1931]*

The small Croatian village called Grice in Ribnik County lies nineteen kilometers (about thirteen miles) northwest of the city of Karlovac. This farming community rests in a loop of the Kupa River on the Slovenian-Croatian border.

Although my physical life began there in 1935, my cultural roots grew from my family and those of many other villagers whose surnames, like my own, eventually would spread to other countries and other continents. I knew many of these people, but the stories of others, some happy and some sad, I learned from my family, especially my father, Janko Bosiljevac, who lived long enough to impress me with the history of our area and its people.

May this memoir help immigrant families and their descendants learn how their ancestors lived before they arrived in America, how that area from which they emigrated looked, why their families left, and why a number of them later returned to their modest homes. During different eras, people emigrated for various reasons, perhaps wars in Europe or because Croatia had always been occupied by foreign powers and Croatians yearned for more opportunities. *(Croatia and Slovenia were parts of Yugoslavia until June 25, 1991, when both declared their independence.)*

My husband Ivan and I decided to leave Croatia a few years after World War II. Although immigration into the United States was rare at that time, we still decided that this country would offer us the best opportunity to work toward a better future for ourselves and our descendants. Almost every household in Ribnik County had at least one family member who emigrated to North America during the 19th and 20th centuries.

During the 1990's, I worked with many immigrants for a Croatian charity organization. Many of these people have told me they regret not having learned more from their families -- about what life was like over there, what the places looked like, what happened to their friends and neighbors. This book is for those people, and for my descendants, as well. I don't want them to realize one day that they, too, have an unfulfilled curiosity about Croatia, its customs, and the families from which they had come. Through my life experiences and those of my parents, grandparents and generations before them, perhaps our homeland can live on in the memories of these immigrants' families.

Table of Contents

Chapter   Page

1. The Long Dry Summer — 9
2. Families of Grice — 31
3. Seasons of Our Lives — 55
4. Families of Golivrh — 73
5. "Our Little Croatian Corner" — 93
6. World War II Reaches Us — 109
7. Two Kinds of Wolves — 127
8. Marriage and Escape — 141
9. Our Unusual Route to America — 161
10. A Change in Lifestyle — 173
11. All That Glitters Is Not Paris — 187
12. We Adapt — 195
13. America: Here We Come! — 205
14. New World – New Experiences — 215
15. Ivan's Dream Comes True — 221
16. . . . and So Does Mine — 229
17. Croatia Is Reborn — 239
18. Life's Circular Journey — 253

Lipnik County Surnames — 267
Other Family Memorabilia — 269

Chapter 1: **The Long Dry Summer**

Life in Ribnik County and in our village Grice was hard and busy during summer, but also enjoyable for those who loved nature and a clean, healthy environment. Houses in Grice were scattered, some on the hill and some down by a highway in the lowlands. Farther down the highway lay a deeper valley in which our spring was located. This spring supplied water for Grice and the neighboring village of Veselice.

From my mother, who was eager to tell me stories as she worked, I learned about the year 1935, when Grice had a hot, dry summer. During spring and normal summers, she remembered, the valley and surrounding area looked like a real paradise. At the water's source, people of the two villages had built a dome where pure, sparkling water rose from the depths, splashing into many small pebbles. People from the two villages built a twenty-foot long concrete trough in which the ladies washed their clothes until all the dirt disappeared, with hardly a speck of soap remaining. Above the dome towered tall trees. On the other side of the dome were luscious green grasses, wild flowers and flowering bushes. Another stream connected with ours, gurgling down over large rocks and settling down onto level ground. From there it slowly murmured away from Grice and then past Veselice. Even more springs and creeks flowed through Ribnik County and into the Kupa River.

During normal summers when there was enough rain, people approaching from up the hill could hear the sound of water as it flowed down between large rocks into the otherwise quiet valley. In 1935, however, this beautiful spring which for years had supplied water to the local people dried up, causing continuous suffering. There was no murmuring of water. There was no washing of clothes. There was no drinking water! Once in a while desperate women would come to see if there was any water, but usually they found only dry pebbles. When a little water appeared the women, including my mother who was expecting a baby in three months, struggled to carry back four gallons each on their heads.

With his neighbors, my father traveled down the highway about four miles to the village of Ribnik, stopping at Obrh Creek near the famous castle in which the family of Zrinski and Frankopani had lived a long time before. This lovely castle, large and round in the center, was designed for the aristocratic family as a defense against the Turks who plundered Croatia and Bosnia from the 15th to the 18th centuries.

(Ribnik Castle)

Since the aristocrats disappeared, the castle has belonged to the county of Ribnik. Authorities have since used the castle for their offices as well as for various activities including dances, classes for young people and some theatrical shows.   Once in a while young people from America whose families had roots in Ribnik came to the castle to perform for area residents.

In the summer of 1935, however, my father and his friends had not gone there to enjoy the beauty of Ribnik's castle and its surrounding property. Fortunately for them and other local residents, Obrh Creek, with its own millhouse nearby, never dried up. It was located within one hundred feet of the castle. Lined up at this creek were people from the hillside, gratefully filling their barrels. When they returned to their homes, not a drop in those barrels was wasted.

The people of Grice were very grateful for the efforts that had brought drinking water, but that summer had also been extremely bad for crops as well as for people. Nobody had enough homegrown food to last the entire year as they usually had in rainy summers. In that era, people in the European countryside depended on their land for food to sustain them through the entire year. During a rainless summer such as 1935, food supplies became short so people were forced to buy food . . .but buying food was a problem. People didn't have any paying jobs other than farming their own lands.

There was a little help, however. Almost every family in Ribnik County owned a parcel of the forest which stretched to the southwest of the villages. Selling wood from their forest parcels to city people who needed to warm their apartments gave farmers some money to fund their own urgent needs. Some fortunate people had wells; these were usually people who returned from America where they had saved some of their hard earned money to use when they came back home.

Finally the hot, dry summer ended. As the weather turned frigid, I came into the world at house No. 7 on Brdo on Tuesday, November 19, 1935. My parents, Janko and Marija (Jagas) Bosiljevac named me Ana Bosiljevac, the same name as my grandmother. I was baptized by Father Alojz Springer at Saint Ilija Catholic Church, beneath the Lipnik, in the presence of my aunt and godmother, Barbara Savor, my mother's sister. My step-grandmother helped my mother during my birth. No doctors or nurses were present. Grandma Kata had no children of her own, but she helped deliver all of my mother's babies, as well as most of the babies in the neighborhood.

But Grandma Kata was not so happy when she saw I was a girl. Her neighbors asked her, "What did your family get?" and she answered "an old maid." The neighbors could tell that Grandma was disappointed. Nevertheless, she loved me even though I was a girl. When my family debated what name to give me, my parents said, 'Let's name her after Granma Kata." But Grandma Kata said, 'That wouldn't be fair. Let's give her the name of her real grandma, Ana." Ana was my father's mother, who died when my father was only one month old. Her name was Ana (Jarmek) Bosiljevac. When I married, I became Ana (Bosiljevac) Jarmek.

When my cousin was born her grandmother asked the ladies who helped deliver the child, "What did my family and I get – a boy or a girl?" They answered, "You and the Jarnevic family got a little girlie." The grandmother then asked, "Would you please look again? Maybe it isn't a girlie." All of us laughed a long time over that remark, but she loved her granddaughter Barbara the same as if she were a boy.

My mother's first child was a girl named Ljubica, born December 13, 1932. I had always wanted a sister, but my parents told me only how pretty a child she was. My sister died when she was eleven months old. Neither doctors nor medicine was easy to come by at that time; therefore many children (and older people too) died unnecessarily.

My parents' second child was a boy born February 28, 1934. Drago was better news for my grandmother who delivered him.

(Left: Drago with   his   wife Ana.)

I was born after Drago, although Grandma, of course, still had hoped for another boy.

(Right: Jure with his wife Ana.)

My brother Jure, the last child in our family, was born three years after me on November 12, 1938. A week later Aunt Dragica, my father's sister, took him to church to record his birth and have him baptized. When the priest asked her when the child had been born, she didn't remember so she simply said, "Yesterday." Since "yesterday" was November 17, 1938, that is the date on Jure's birth certificate. Dragica wasn't thinking of my brother's future when she said it, but for his entire life Jure has been disturbed by this wrong birth date on his certificate.

Croatians, as you see, looked at girls as burdens to the family, but there was a practical reason why we females weren't welcome: For a daughter's marriage her parents were obligated to give a bedroom set to the newlyweds, as well as presents to the groom's family, with whom the bride and groom would live. An even greater expense was also involved: The bride's parents had to give their daughter either a section of the family's property or money to pay off the property where she had been born. Most small farmers struggled to pay off their daughter's portion of their land when she married. Some people brought money from America. For them it was easier. The poor just gave a parcel of land that they greatly needed for themselves.

When my mother married my father, she got nothing. Her father said, "I have six children left in my house to feed. I can't give my daughter anything now, but I will later when I accumulate some money." He never saved enough to pay off my mother, so my father and his parents just let it go. When my grandfather Jagas died, the court conducted a hearing to settle the inheritances of his children who hadn't been paid off for property, but my mother wouldn't take anything. She said, "I am leaving my part to my sister Dragica who took care of our parents before they died."

Not every daughter would do that. Our next-door neighbors had a different experience with their girls who, many years after they got married carved up their parents' property. Then they sold it and emigrated to Canada. They left that poor family, Josip and Mara Gojmerac and their six children, in even worse poverty

14

than they had been before. When Mara's father learned of their misery, he brought them to Argentina where he had immigrated when Mara was a small child.

In his eighties during World War II, our grandfather was seldom in a good mood. But when he cheered up, he would tell us children of the things he learned in that faraway country, America. He had gone there three times: first to Pittsburgh, Pennsylvania, then two times to Kansas City, Kansas. He stayed five years each time, although, he told us, "Each trip one way would cost me one year of work there." When he returned to Croatia he would purchase some land for the family, but he never was able to make enough to build up his savings.

At that time he and his wife Ana had six children, three boys and three girls. Their first child, a daughter Ljuba, was born in 1886 while grandpa was in Pittsburgh, Pennsylvania. Daughter Barbara was born in 1891, followed by two sons, Marko in 1893 and Ivan in 1895. Reluctantly, Grandpa returned to America, this time finding work in Kansas City, Kansas, and returning to Croatia in 1900. Daughter Dragica was born in 1902 and son Izidor in 1904, so their family had grown to eight.

Grandpa's brother Juro had seven members in his family, brother Nikola had three, and their cousin Josip had three in his. All of these people in my grandpa's family lived in House No. 5. Twenty-one people lived in the main house. Each family had their own small house where they would sleep or stay when they needed to be alone, but they still ate together in the main house. Could anyone live like that today? Perhaps not, but Grandpa said they all got along just fine.

When Grandpa returned from America the second time, he brought back some money and suggested that they split their farm and build separate houses for each family. Cousin Josip stayed in No. 5, brother Nikola built House No. 6, Grandfather Tomo built House No. 7, and his brother Juro built House No. 8. Before the split, Brdo had only five houses, but afterwards Brdo had eight family homes. So, my grandfather's family then had one half of the houses in Brdo. *(House #7 below.)*

Houses in our county were built mostly out of wood, but differently than those here in America. Inside, we had wooden floors and wooden ceilings, and the walls, with small windows, were finished with stucco. Toilet facilities were outside on the back of the house. A porch often led to both sides of the home. The kitchen extended through the wall to the living room in order to spread the heat through the house from the clay stove on which the women cooked meals. The main house also had wood stoves, but they cooled during the nights, so in the morning it was very cold to get up, especially for the first person who was responsible for restarting the fire in the stoves. At our home, that person was my grandma, and after her death, my mother. Most families had a smaller building, separate from the house, where a son and daughter-in-law could sleep and have some privacy. There was no heat in these small

16

buildings, however, so sometimes the young couple would move back to the main house in the winter.

Such homes were built with very little money, but we were self-sufficient. The people in the community came together to help as each family built their house.

Early in the 20th Century, my grandfather had built his home. Today, 100 years later, the house still stands there for my brothers to use when they return for a visit. As repairs are needed, they usually just recover the walls which are still holding up well. They are made of oak and chestnut -- hard woods -- four inches thick. Originally the roof was covered with straw, but in 1957, the family replaced it with tiles that are still there. Beneath that house is a basement which allows air to circulate to prevent mold.

(House No. 7 remodeled)

With the building of the last three homes, Brdo had a total of eight families with about fifty family members.

All of them had the last name Bosiljevac, and many of them had the same first names, as well.

How that happened is an interesting story in Croatian history: Under Hungarian rule, many Croatians left populated areas for new, uncultivated land where they could live and farm. *(It is most likely that the people who settled in Grice had come from the Zagorje region since the names and languages are similar.)*

In Grice, however, aristocratic authorities migrated with the farmers. The aristocrats settled the six farm families into six different places in Grice. They awarded the best land and the entire forest to themselves and gave to the six families some poorer land on which to live. Besides working their own farms, however, those six families had to work for free on the lord's land.

Local families were obligated to their lords for providing at least one family member to perform such labor. If someone didn't show up as arranged, authorities would bring the person to their castle where he or she received twenty-five lashes. Under Hungarian governance, that was the law. My great-grandma Jarmek told her family how in the mornings she used to walk to work for those lords while combing her hair on the way. She had no time to take care of herself since she took care of her family and worked for those lords.

Older generations told the younger how the first Brdo settler was an older girl whose last name was Bosiljevac. Many people blamed her for their hard lives on that steep hill as they toiled to raise crops there and had to carry water back from our spring in the valley.

I often wondered, if a woman named Bosiljevac was the first settler in Brdo, why did the generations after she married still carry her surname and not that of the man she married? Well, the history of the rule of the Hungarian lords governing Croatia established that custom. I learned how my own family had preserved the Bosiljevac name even though they had only a daughter named Ana (my grandpa's grandma), who married Mato Car on April 12, 1818. Mato Car couldn't keep his last name because he came to live with his wife's family in Brdo. My paternal grandfather was known as Tomo Car-Bosiljevac. Eventually a new law permitted residents to choose only one last name, so my family chose Bosiljevac, as that had been the original name of Brdo.

That law was enforced not only in Grice, but in the whole Croatian countryside. I never heard the reason for it; perhaps it allowed local lords to more easily keep track of the families who worked free for them day after day.

That law also was evident in other members of our family. When my grandfather's uncle Miho got married, his bride's name was Ana Secen. Miho's son Josip also married a girl named Ana Secen, as did Grandpa's brother Juro. When Uncle Miho died, Grandpa's brother Nikola married Miho's widow Ana. My grandfather, the youngest of them all, perhaps couldn't find his own "Ana Secen," so he stopped in a place named "Jarmek Valley" where he found his bride, Ana Jarmek. It must have become interesting when all of those relatives and their wives lived together in House No. 5! All four women had the first name Ana, and three of the four had the maiden name of Secen. These were not related, but they all had come from the same place, "Secen's Valley." So, most of the population of Secen's Valley has the last name Secen.

Life on those small farms was hard, and few of us would want to live like that now (*although even today, people who work usually live better than those who do not.*) So, we in those days were better off to work hard, keep our modest homes and grow our own food. These gave us security for survival.

Even when we children were small, we were reminded of America every day of our lives, not only by our grandfather, but by many other people in our small community who had gone to that country and then returned. Those who had stayed in America for a greater length of time brought a lot of money home to their families, and also brought us English words which we mixed with our native Croatian. When Alojz Secen's father returned from America he told his neighbors that in America a man is called "Mister." After that he, his son and his grandson were called by their nickname – Mister.

Grandfather taught us children some English words including how to count. In his old age, he liked to be reminded of America. Whether cooped up in winter or outside during our warm summers, we would gather close around him in the house or on the front porch to listen to him reminisce about the experiences he had during his years across the ocean. He told us about the Armour Packing House where he had worked with many people from Ribnik county. He felt right at home living in Kansas City and working with people from the same place he came from. Living conditions there, however, were often not much better than in Grice. The workers rented houses without heat, without water, and without an indoor toilet. Although missing their families, most men felt that at least they were making some money which they couldn't do back home.

After my grandfather built his new house, and after his fifth and sixth children were born, it was time for him to make more money in America. On June 23, 1907, he arrived for the third time at Ellis Island. This time he lived with his oldest child, Louise Mlinaric, and her husband in Escanaba, Michigan.

Louise cooked meals for her own family, including her father Tomo. To earn money she also cooked for a few other men. Grandpa told us a story of how Louise once

20

played cards while cooking a meal for those people and ended up burning the meal. Grandpa Tomo criticized Louise because he believed that she was too young for such responsibilities, but her husband came to her defense and told his father-in-law, "She is my responsibility now. I am her husband. You have no right to criticize her."

Grandfather left Louise and her husband and came to Kansas City, where he found many people from the same place where he was born. In 1908 his son Marko arrived in Kansas City at the age of sixteen. Marko was married in 1913 to Mary Sambol, whose family came from the village of Ribnik. Marko and Mary had two daughters, Ana (nee Bosiljevac) Ropar and Mary (nee Bosiljevac) Zukel.

(As you will see, these two names – "Ana" and "Mary" – have followed me in my life. I have never figured out why.)

Grandpa's third child, Ivan, arrived in Kansas City in 1911. Ivan married a girl named Mary Sopcic. When my father, Janko, got married in Croatia nineteen years later, his wife's name also was Mary. Three brothers all had married Marys. When I married, two of my husband's brothers married girls named Ana, and all three of us had mothers whose names were "Mary" 'I have two brothers who both have wives named "Ana."

Grandfather returned home to Croatia in 1912 from his third and last trip to America. His last child, Janko (John) was born on October 2, 1913, when Grandpa and Grandma were both fifty years old.

Janko, my father, had bad luck right from birth. When he was one month old, his mother Ana became very ill. With no fast transportation available, Grandpa and his friends took Ana to the hospital in a farm wagon pulled by oxen. It took them four hours to get to Karlovac. A few minutes before they arrived, Ana died.

Her death was, of course, a shock to my grandfather. Not only had he lost his wife, but he was left with three children including baby Janko, who now had nothing to eat. There were no baby formulas nor any other good things but cow's milk available. On that very day, as his wife lay dead, my grandpa's four sisters pressured him to marry a widow named Kata whom he had never met. His sisters had never met Kata either, but they had heard of her. Grandpa got upset at his sisters for even suggesting this thing at such a difficult time. They told him, "We understand your feelings, but children have to eat. Somebody has to cook meals for you and those two older children, and somebody has to feed the baby."

Grandpa rejected his sisters' idea. After one of his sisters took Janko to her house to care for him with her own children, he tried coping with the two older kids, who weren't much help at home. One evening, when the children asked him for food that he didn't have, he realized how helpless he was. He didn't know what to do. Working his farm and preparing meals for his children, which he had never done before, was too much. He couldn't cope with the situation any more. It was too soon for him to consider marrying the widow Kata. That evening his head spun.

If any of us came to find ourselves in that same situation, we might at first blame God, asking ourselves why he had put us in such a position with no way out. We might wonder what we had done to deserve this. Perhaps all of us might think these things, just as my grandfather did.

God, however, understands our pain when we need Him. He understood my grandfather's pain at that desperate time. . .

Someone knocked on grandfather's door. Being a religious man, he thought that God might have sent an angel to help him. God did indeed send someone. It wasn't an angel; it was Ivan Jernevic, the godfather of his children. He had brought Grandpa and his children food. He advised him to be patient. Then he told his friend to heed the advice of his four sisters, and take the widow Kata for his wife. "Set your feelings aside," Ivan told my grandfather. "The important thing is to get a new mother for your children." Grandpa realized that he wasn't able to live alone with his children, so he agreed. Grandpa didn't know Kata because she wasn't from Grice or even Ribnik county; she was from Modospotok, a village in Netretic county.

When Kata arrived, she brought baby Janko from Grandfather's sister's house, although he was barely alive. Kata had no children of her own, so marrying this widower gave her the opportunity to mother a child, a need that helped fill her life. She fed Janko cow's milk, spoonful by spoonful until his health returned.

(Above: My father Janko 7 yrs; his father Tomo; back on left, Stepmother Kata; and sister Dragico, 18 yrs.)

With Kata's help, the family situation at home got better, but the following year more difficulty occurred. One day in 1914, ten-year-old Izidor came home from the pasture with the family cows, complaining of a sore throat. His stepmother, Kata, was cooking cornmeal, and the boy asked her to give him food so he could push down something stuck in his throat. Kata began to cry right away, knowing that other children with these symptoms had died in a few days. I think they called it the Spanish Flu. Unfortunately, Kata was right. A few days later Izidor died.

At that time, on the brink of World War I, no one was going to America to work. Since his return home to Croatia Grandfather hadn't heard anything about the three children whom he had left in America back in 1912.

In October 1913, my father Janko had been born, and his mother Ana had died later that year. In the same month father's older brother Marko, who was in Kansas City, got married. Marko had no way to hear of the problems that were devastating his family back in Grice.

(Above at right: My father's brother, Marko Bosiljevac, visiting Croatia from Kansas City in 1956; his sister Dragica behind him, her husband Vinko Dimic left, and his daughter Sofia, center.)

24

Grandpa's daughter Dragica, who was then fifteen years old, married seventeen-year-old Miho Svazic. Both of them were still like children and shouldn't have married, but families pushed these two young people into it. When Dragica lost her mother Ana, the family believed she would have a hard time marrying someone as she got older -- at least that is what people thought back then. Soon after Miho and Dragica were married, they had a baby girl.

After the baby was born, however, Miho immigrated to Canada. He evidently "forgot" he had a family back in Croatia because he later got married in Hamilton.

Dragica couldn't stay with Miho's parents when her husband left her and his child, so she went to Zagreb to work for a family who had a greenhouse in which they grew vegetables. She worked there until she retired. Dragica remarried a nice and handsome widower, Vinko Dimic. He had three children of his own, but together they had no children. Dragica's daughter Ana still lives in the Croatian capital city of Zagreb.

Grandfather was the only one of his brothers and sisters who worked in America. Some of his nieces and nephews, however, did immigrate, mostly to Kansas City. The generations still living in Kansas City have the surnames Bosiljevac, Novosel, Dolinar, Mus, Zugecic, Nastav, Jadric, Ivicak. Others are farther generations. Some of them don't know I am from their family.

My grandpa's two brothers had to change their last names when they moved in with their wives' families because by Hungarian law, which applied to Croatia, this had to be done by men who lived with their wives' families. Grandpa's brother Janko changed his last name to Mus. His other brother, Josip, changed his to Jarnevic.

Living in Grice as a small child, I never realized that my step-grandmother was not my father's real mother. She was good to us children, but she wasn't to my mother. Kata had raised my father as her own son, but when he got married, she thought my mother had taken him away from her, that he wasn't paying enough attention to her. The same things happen to other daughters-in-law as well. Most of those people on small farms to which their sons brought new wives to live couldn't accept the women as family members. To the families they remained outsiders. That was hard on young couples who had to live with their parents.

Grandma Kata and the woman next door, also named Kata (who happened to be the wife of my grandfather's nephew), never got along peacefully. As I look back on it, the relationship between those two ladies was entertaining.

Grandpa's family of twenty-one members had been able to live peacefully in one house, but that was before Kata and the other Kata joined the group. Kata and Kata lived three hundred feet from each other, but that was too close for peace to exist between them. They argued all the time about their chickens, sheep, goats and cattle entering each other's yards.

Grandpa told us about something that happened before I was born. It was Grandpa that time who was involved instead of Grandma Kata. Grandpa saw his neighbor Kata's goats trampling his young, beautiful fruit tree. When he complained to neighbor Kata, she replied, "My goats never entered your yard or did anything to your trees!" She would never admit to any wrong doing. Kata was not afraid of my Grandpa, so she got up close to him to tell him that he was wrong. That did it. Grandpa lost his temper; he grabbed her neck and started to choke her.

Kata was scared, but she wasn't going to let him get off so easily. When she had collected her thoughts, Kata went to the county courthouse to sue Grandpa. On her way down the highway near Novosel Valley where Kata was born, she met a former neighbor who asked where she was going. Kata replied, "I am going to court to sue my neighbor Tomo who almost chocked me to death." She told her former neighbor the story but denied any responsibility. The old neighbor, however, knew Kata and thought he knew what had probably happened. He told her, "Kata, go back to your home. The authorities at the courthouse may not think you're entirely innocent either." So, Kata thought for a long moment, and returned home.

I was little, but I remember the arguments outside our houses. Still, the women always talked. I remember once when neighbor women gathered at the beautiful yard of House No. 5, the original Bosiljevac family home, when no one lived here anymore. The spot was visible by the entire neighborhood, so usually on Sunday afternoons, Malca Bosiljevac arrived first. Then the others followed. This gathering is what passed for the weekly social life in the busy lives of ladies from Brdo.

During World War II, the neighbor, Kata, brought her great-grandson who had just started to walk. Grandma Kata was also there, listening to every word spoken by neighbor Kata. The ladies watched little Janko starting to walk down the hill, bobbling back and forth. After watching him successfully make his way down to the bottom of the hill without falling, the proud great-grandmother, Kata the neighbor, said, "Look at my Janko! He is strong and handsome as was my husband Peter when he was alive."

Grandma Kata couldn't let it go, of course, without saying something. "Oh, my neighbor, Kata. If you think your husband Peter was handsome to you, he also was handsome to everybody else." Everybody burst into laughter because they knew how the two Katas could irritate each other. Other neighbor ladies might argue as well, but arguments between those two Katas were funny, and then they would speak to each other as if nothing had happened just a few minutes before.

Such memories of the Katas are indeed amusing to me still, but it is the pictures in my mind of Grandpa Tomo that dominate my childhood memories.

Thirty years after Grandpa returned to Croatia for good he still kept some of the things he brought back from America. I used to watch him open a large trunk out of which he would bring his possessions from America. He would just admire these mementos, keeping them in the trunk as souvenirs. Most of all I remember a cigar box in which he kept some of his important documents and money. (At that time he didn't have much of the latter.)

His most cherished possession was his smoking pipe, which he lost in our small forest when he was clearing out some debris. Whenever something bothered Grandpa, he would just walk around silently, breathing out a deep "hoo" sound while exhaling. Grandma would notice, "Tomo, I know something is wrong by that 'hoo' sound." Usually he would not tell her what was bothering him. We children felt sorry to see him so sad, so we begged him to tell us what was wrong. When he admitted that he had lost his last smoking pipe, the one he had brought back from America, we ran into the forest and searched all over. We wanted to find it so we could put a smile back on his face. That would have made us happy as well, but unfortunately, our search was in vain. Grandfather had lost his best reminder of America, the America he would never forget.

My family's roots are of great significance to me. I am very grateful that my father, John, has given me much of the information I've needed to put our family stories down on paper. I have always been interested in where these relatives originated and how they lived.

What could be more important than for people to know their families' roots and how they lived far back in time? We appreciate life better when we know how the past generations lived. When their lives prove to have been harder and poorer, may we be more grateful for what we have and more sympathetic to those who live still in poverty.

Chapter 2: **Families of Grice**

Memories of growing up in this small Croatian village will always be with me –- many which made me happy and others less pleasant that I am reluctant to think too much about. I was twenty-one years old when I left, and because of the comfortable way in which I live now, it is difficult, almost unbelievable, to think about how my family and others lived then.

My childhood years were very happy. I had no idea what life could look like elsewhere. We had to survive and eat that which we had produced with only manual farming equipment, without electricity at home, with no water piped in and sometimes with no water at all unless we could bring it from a distance. In addition to our daily hardships, there were wars in Europe. Between them most Europeans lived without luxuries, especially those of us who lived in small countries constantly under the domination of larger ones. Maybe the breathtaking beauty of nature around us gave us our energy to appreciate life as it was for us.

I don't look at the place in which I was born with anger or sadness, however. A nature-loving child, I enjoyed all around me immensely.   I embraced the world's beauty, no matter whether it was summer or winter and cherish the good memories instead. In my mind, I can still walk through the narrow paths between fields covered with lovely green crops and remember how the winds made them wave under nice sunny skies. I see fruit trees which could let ripe treasures drop into our hands, full of sweetness through the summer and fall.

Many people were happy there despite the hard life we all had. My grandfather never complained, even though he knew what life was like in the America he visited. Of course, it wasn't too much better in America during that time, but still there was more opportunity there than on those small farms where we lived.

Even though her life was often extremely hard, my mother loved Grice and the land on which our crops grew. But my father was never happy; during frequent visits to his sister, he saw a better life in the city where she lived. When father worked the fields with oxen and plow, he became irritated and sometimes raged when the plow hit a rock. At age thirty-five, with three teenage children, he thought that was it -- he would never have an opportunity for a better life than the one he had in Grice. Older men had the chance to go to America where they could make some money to bring home for their families' desperate need, but men of my father's age couldn't, because World War II erupted in Europe, and the doors to America closed. After the war, that door closed even more tightly because communists were taking over Yugoslavia. Communists let young people work in cities for small wages and gave them free education, but there was a "catch" attached to that privilege – they indoctrinated these young people in their communist ideas.

As a child I understood little of the political problems in our country. For my father, however, politics provided an intellectual outlet from his farm labor. Whenever he had the opportunity to discuss politics with other men, the conversation showed his intense interest. I enjoyed listening to these discussions, even though I understood very little. When I was about eight years old, I could hardly read at all, but, like my mother's entire family I liked books. Once I grabbed two books which my parents were reading. They were filled with tiny letters and hundreds of pages, but nothing to interest me. They were books of politics, but far too difficult for me. Even the few poems in them were too complicated for me, which made me very sad. I remember only a picture of Stjepan Radic on the first page and one of his brother Anton on the opposite page. When I turned the page, there was Saint Peter's cathedral in Rome and one in Zagreb, Croatia. The Radic brothers were leaders of the peasant party in Croatia following World War I. Recently, when my father and I had a conversation about the Radic brothers he said, "I wonder what happened to those two books during the war." With a little smile on my face I told him, "Mother hid them under the wine press on the porch because she was afraid the partisans would find them and punish us."

Our younger generation looked to grab any opportunity for a better future, and so one by one they disappeared from the countryside, including that of Grice. They settled in our cities where they got some kind of government job, but wages were hardly enough to feed themselves. They thought there was no hope for their parents who were too old to leave their homes and settle in the cities; so they had to be left behind, most of them until the end of their lives.

Sometimes, however, a change becomes possible: I was able to bring my parents from Grice to America at a better time than when my grandfather Tomo had been here many years earlier.

I was a nature-loving child who enjoyed all around me immensely. I embraced nature's beauty, no matter whether it was summer or winter. Most people complain about snow and cold weather. I do, too, now that I am older, but when I was young, snow and icicles were as interesting as were those colorful blue jays flying over the snow. Since we didn't know any better life existed, we used the beauty of nature to make us happy.

Although our land was difficult to cultivate, life would have been easier if our Croatia had been independent. What we needed most was better roads, piped water, electricity and telephones. When I lived there, none of those were provided, either from a government authority or a private company. We also needed some kind of small shops where people could make some money for their desperate needs.

Most of us young people who left following World War II were able to establish better lives for ourselves and our children. However, I hope all who left remember also the good things we had in Croatia, rather than only those difficulties which pushed us to leave.

A question continues to rise in my mind: <u>What</u> history did we leave? Grice was a village established by people with just six surnames: Car, Novosel, Bosiljevac, Jarmek, Secen and Fabac.

Only one family named Car settled in Grice, at a place they called Car's Valley which grew through the years to fifteen families while I was there. My father's great-grandfather was from Car's Valley. Some people from Car's Valley immigrated right here to Kansas City. Three of my grandfather's sisters had married men in Car's Valley. One sister's daughter, named Franca (Fabac) Novosel immigrated to Kansas City where she had two sons named Peter and Mike and two daughters named Mary and Louise. Some deceased members of the Car family can be found in our cemetery in Kansas City, Kansas.

My favorite place in Car's Valley was the Kralj family home. My family had a parcel of our land right by their house, and I loved to go with my family to work the land. My family would send me to that house to bring us water from their well. Usually an older lady named Dragica was home, and I would have to ask her for water. She was always happy to fill up my two-liter bottle, but I would turn away fast before she could ask me any questions. I was a shy girl when I met someone not from my neighborhood. Dragica's son Mike and his family immigrated to Toronto, Canada.

The Kralj family had one beautiful place on a small elevation from which they had a view of the entire Grice Village and other villages in Ribnik County. That place was located right by the property of our aristocratic family, which they had chosen as the best when they settled there. **(This photo shows, at right side, the road to Upper Grice.)**

About one fourth of a mile from Car's Valley is another small place named Novosel's Valley after the first settlers who came there. That small area in which ten families lived was on a flat surface right by the highway. Our beautiful valley with springs and the creek were just on the other side of the highway.

Many people from Novosel's Valley emigrated to different countries. Some of the Novosels settled right here in Kansas City. Today we can find their names in our cemetery on State Avenue and 38th Street.

In our imaginations now, we leave Novosel Valley for our slow climb to upper Grice. There on upper Grice we find four small places where the families of Bosiljevac, Jarmek, Secen and Fabac settled. When we turn at  the Majer intersection, we rest our legs on the level ground for about 300 feet. Then we have a sharp climb to Brdo where for two decades Bosiljevac families lived in houses 1-8.

The first house belonged to Janko and Franca Bosiljevac. Janko died before I could remember him, but Franca (Secen) Bosiljevac told me many stories of her life when she was young. When Janko returned from making money in America, he met Franca at the Majer intersection. Janko was engaged at the time to my aunt Ljuba, my grandfather's first child. According to my family, even before Janko left for America, Franca disrupted Janko and Ljuba's plans by coming to Janko's land to harvest hazelnuts.

In those years, young people over there didn't date for long periods before they married. It was sufficient only to see each other and decide if there was an attraction between them. Apparently that is what happened to Janko and Franca. She remembers that when Janko returned from America, their first meeting was again on that Majer intersection. She smiled as she told us, "When I saw him nicely dressed in American clothes, tilting his American hat to one side, my heart had to wait for him. My dreams came true when he put gentle hands on my shoulder and said, 'Franca, my love, would you marry me?'"

As Franca told us that story, she laughed at how times had changed since she was young. That meeting and another when she came to pick up those hazelnuts were enough for the two of them to fall in love. Janko told Franca, "Tonight I will come to your home, accompanied by someone, to ask your parents if they will give me permission to marry you."

Having a friend come with him was important. That person would help him ask the girl's parents how much they would give for their daughter's marriage (to pay off her property). That was important because when a daughter leaves, her part of the family property goes with her. Franca rushed back home to warn her parents to be prepared for guests that night. People called that occasion "Uprosi," which meant "ask for marriage."

Janko and Franca were married, and their first child, Milka, was born soon after. As was the custom when a young couple married, they usually had their first child, then the husband would go to America, leaving his family with parents or siblings. Janko stayed in America for ten years, returning in 1912, the same year as did my grandpa Tomo. That was the last time for both of them to see America.

In 1913, the couple had another daughter named Ljuba, the same year my grandparents had a boy Janko, who was to become my father.

As World War I erupted, nobody could return to America, so many of those men who had come to see their families had to stay there, like it or not. Janko and Franca had two more daughters, Dora and Ana. When Milka was fifteen, her parents let her marry Ivan Tomecalj from the village of Srbelje by the Kupa River She and her parents were on top of the world when Milka began her new life in such a convenient area where she had plenty of water and good fertile land there on the Slovenian border.

(Photo above: Milka [Bosiljevac] Tomecalj)

(We from upper land called those people down on level surfaces "Poljci," which means "the people of the plain." They called us "Brigovci," the people of the hillside. Lucky villages were those down by the Kupa River: Paka, Artic, Sracak, Mosenci, Jadrici, Zaluka and Pravutina. There were others on level ground, but they weren't next to the river.)

When Milka (Bosiljevac) Tomecalj began her life with Ivan, however, he did what her father had done when he married Franca. When their son was born, Ivan was on his way to America. Although their land was better than ours, they needed money the same as we did. Milka had lived ten years without her father, but her son never knew his father, even though he did send money home.

There were, of course, reasons why many men never returned home. They worked hard here without their families, but many were also weak and often let themselves be taken either by alcohol or other women.

Ivan's son Janko married a girl named Mara in the early 1940's. They had one daughter, Milica. When Ivan got sick in Pittsburgh, Pennsylvania, he asked his wife Milka to come live with him after the war. When she arrived in America, the couple moved to Kansas City where they had some relatives. Ivan got sicker, so they moved to Arizona's warmer climate, but that didn't help him either. They returned to Kansas City where he died. Milka later remarried, but that husband also died.

During the late 50's, people were sneaking out of communist Yugoslavia, so Milka's granddaughter Milica **(Milica [Tomecalj] Sambol above)** crossed the border to Italy. From there she was able to immigrate to Kansas City, joining her grandma Milka. America's population has always grown because immigrants like the Croatians have fled there to find an opportunity to raise their families without oppression and poverty.

Like other of Ribnik County's youth who had settled in Kansas City, so did young Joe Sambol, whom Milica married during the early 60's. Joe had been born and grew up in Ribnik Village. Their family home was on the spot from which they had a view of the historical castle and Obrh Creek.

Milica's parents arrived in Kansas City in the 60's. Their little farm in Srbelje was abandoned and still is. It was a nice location with fertile land and plenty of water, but not many people are willing to live that kind of life any more. They leave to move either to cities or to different countries.

Janko and Franca's daughter Ljuba had also married at age fifteen to twenty-year-old Mato Hadusek. Both he and Ljuba's parents made the mistake of pushing this tiny girl into marriage before she was ready either for a husband or for life in the husband's home.

(At right: Ljuba [Bosiljevac] Hadusek and husband Mato.)

When I was a teenager, Ljuba and her mother visited us occasionally during winter days when we were free of farm duty. The men were usually out of the house, cutting wood in the forest or just strolling through the forest for fresh air, but we women would talk as we kept busy weaving or knitting. I was always eager to hear the ladies' life stories. That was when I learned how people lived when my parents or grandparents were younger.

Both Ljuba and Franca were funny. Ljuba related the sad story of her marriage to Mato, who never had any romantic date with his bride-to-be. Their wedding was in the family's house as was common for every couple in our community. Franca had been proud when her daughter married so young, but Ljuba gave us a different impression: "As guests began to leave the house, I wanted to leave with them. I asked my father-in-law to take me back home, but he said that my home was now at their house with my husband.

"About that time Mato undressed in the living room and walked in his underwear toward our cold bedroom where the bedroom furniture my parents gave me had been set up. Mato noticed how restrained I was, so he said if I wished to follow him he would be there in our bedroom. I knew then I had no choice, but going into that room I grabbed two pillows and set them on a dresser which was large enough for me to use as a bed. When Mato saw my dramatic behavior, he jumped out of bed, grabbed me and the two pillows and threw me to our bed. He then left, going to another room where he slept every night for two months before his call to army duty. He was in the army for more than a year, but by the time he came home, I was stronger and more mature, so our actual married life began at that time."

When Ljuba's two sisters got married and left their parents' home, she returned with her husband Mato to live at Brdo with her parents at house No. 1 where she was born. Their first son, Ljubek, was born January 9, 1934, the same year as my brother Drago. They became best friends. Their second son, Mirko, was born May 17, 1939. He became the best friend of my brother Jure.

During the 1960's and 70's, Croatians like Mirko and other Europeans entered the German work force in massive numbers to rebuild the country's destruction during WWII. As Ribnik County was only about a five-hour drive by car from Munich, many of our people worked in Germany and were able to return home almost every weekend. Mirko and his family built a beautiful house in Karlovac, close to my brother Drago. In Brdo, house No. 1 fell empty.

As for house No. 2, Stjepan Bosiljevac married Mara Novosel in 1910. One year later she had a baby boy named Ivan. Stjepan was no different from other men. They had the one child before he went to work in St. Louis, Missouri. More than ten years passed before he returned home after WWI with well accumulated money, most of which he deposited in the local bank. During the depression years he lost all of what was in the bank. His only achievement before he lost the rest of it was building a barn and digging a well in which water was captured from the tile roof of the barn.

When Ivan grew up, he married a girl named Ana Jarmek. Her father Janko Jarmek and my grandmother Ana (Jarmek) Bosiljevac were brother and sister. Ana's parents, Janko and Mara Jarmek immigrated to Kansas City, where Ana was born in 1914.

When the first world war began in Europe, American men were sent to be part of it. Just like the other men who had families in America, Janko was afraid of being drafted, worrying about how his family would survive without him. In his case, Mara had one small baby and another was on the way. So, Janko sent his family back to Croatia to live with his mother and cousin Juro. Janko didn't have to go in the service after all, but Mara and the children had to stay in Croatia, at least until the war was over.

After the war, America was in a depression and Janko was concerned about bringing his family back, so he sent money to Mara to build a house where she and the children could live away from cousin Juro. A new house, however, couldn't satisfy Mara, who was wishing nothing else but to get to America where her husband was.

During these depression years, Croatian people were returning home when they lost their jobs overseas. It happened to Bara Fabac, a lady from Grice who was working in America. Mara Jarmek had America constantly on her mind, so when she knew Bara had returned, she wasted no time in paying a visit. She asked Bara if she would sell a passport to her. When Bara agreed, Mara became very excited, thinking that her greatest wish, to return to her husband in Michigan, would turn their lives around. She knew that this procedure wasn't legal, but people were doing it in desperation. Even Bara's return because she had lost her job in America didn't scare Mara. She knew she would be fine as long as she could be with her husband.

When she got the passport, Mara left her daughters, Ana and Kata, with her mother, and she set out for America. One little detail – she never wrote a letter to her husband saying she was coming! During that time her husband, Janko Jarmek, was living with his niece Ljuba (Bosiljevac) Mlinaric, who was my grandfather's first child.

No one knew Mara was coming to America. She arrived when Ljuba was home alone since both her husband and Mara's were at work. Ljuba was, of course, extremely surprised when Mara showed up at her door. When both of them calmed down, they planned a surprise for Janko, who had no idea Mara was coming.

When Janko arrived, Mara sneaked into a bedroom where she hid behind a door. Ljuba allowed Janko to rest only a short time before trying to get him to her bedroom. It wasn't easy to get him up from his chair, so she said, "Uncle Janko, please, would you come to my room to see my dress which I bought today?" Janko replied, "My dear niece, you know that dresses don't interest me." The fun would be spoiled unless she tried again, "But Uncle Janko, you never saw anything like this dress of mine! Please come." Finally he got up from his chair and followed her into her room, and Mara stepped out from behind the door. When he spotted her, he just said, "Mara, are you here dead or alive?" "I am here alive," she replied, "but I bought a passport from Bara Fabac when she returned from America. I hope I will be able to stay here as have many others who came the same way I did."

After fifteen long years of separation, both Janko and Mara were happily together again. Jobs were hard to find for ladies in Ascanaba, Michigan, so the couple came to Kansas City where Janko had a nephew, Marko Bosiljevac, Ljuba's brother. Their family helped them find jobs at the Armour packing house. They were happy working there, among many others from Ribnik County. Although wages were small during that time, without the responsibility of their children, they saved enough money to be happy.

Their older daughter Ana wrote that she had a marriage proposal from Ivan Bosiljevac. Mara had realized her mistake in not bringing her daughters to America, so she wrote Ana, "You can marry Ivan, but if you don't, your father and I would like you and your sister Kata to come to America." Ivan Bosiljevac was rich because that was when his father, Stjepan, brought lots of money from America and before he lost most of it in the Yugoslav bank.

When Ana and her sister didn't come, she and Janko saved $300 and sent it to help Ana. At that time, this amount was worth much more than it is today.

Janko's and Mara's happiness didn't last longer than one year. One day the authorities came to her work place and told her to pack her bags for Croatia in the morning. The couple speculated that some people who worked at Armour's had turned them in, but perhaps the authorities just got suspicious because she and her husband had different last names. All of the dreams which Mara had for herself and her family were suddenly gone, and they were gone forever. After Mara left, Janko started drinking more and more until he destroyed himself with alcohol.

(Below: Mara Jarmek, her two daughters, Ana and Kata, and their families.)

World War II followed the depression, and any type of communication between Mara and Janko was nonexistent. After the war, everybody tried to contact their families, but Janko Jarmek didn't. He really didn't care anymore for anybody or anything. I remember when Mara asked her daughters to take a picture with her to send to Janko. She was hopeful it would wake him up and renew contact, but that was impossible. My uncle, Marko Bosiljevac, was Janko's nephew. Marko's family helped Janko as much as they could, but he died during the late 1950's, here in Kansas City. Since there was no suit for Janko's burial, Marko supplied one.

When Mara was 65 years old, she was entitled to receive one half of Janko's pension. It wasn't much, but it was a great help to her. Poor woman, she didn't last long either; she died of stomach cancer a few years later. As far as anyone in Grice remembers, Mara's was only the second cancer in Grice's people. Mara's life was hard, raising two daughters alone on her small farm. She was even wounded in her yard during WWII, something that could have happened to any of us when, on occasional days, bullets began flying all over our area.

There were, in Ribnik County, many stories of our people who lived separate lives during those years when men left to make money for their families. Some of these men were strong and some weren't. Many of those men brought their families to America. Some of them, however, didn't trust America to be a stable home either, so they kept their families on those farms and lived their own lonely lives with alcohol until they drank themselves to death.

When Ana Jarmek married Ivan Bosiljevac, they had two sons, Janko and Drago. Drago was born November 11, 1935, just one week before me. Drago and I were the only children born that year on Brdo. Because our last name was Bosiljevac, many of us had the same first names, also. Once my father received a traffic ticket from the county office ordering him to appear in court. When he arrived, he asked the authorities why he was there. They said, "You are here because you drove too fast." He asked, "<u>What</u> did I drive too fast?" "You drove a truck too fast." My father assured them that he had never driven anything but a bike in his life. When they realized the mistake, they asked him if he knew another

Janko Bosiljevac, and he replied, "My neighbor who works in Karlovac has the same name as mine."

A much more serious problem arose when his papers and the other Janko's got mixed up by the American consul in Zagreb, Croatia. When I had filed applications for my parents to come to America, mother's papers came, but father's didn't. My father rushed to Zagreb to ask what happened. The authorities looked in the file, and said, "Look for yourself. Janko Bosiljevac went to Pittsburgh, Pennsylvania, USA one year ago." Father explained that the other man was his neighbor, whose wife was also named Mara, the same as father's wife, and that his parents, whose names were Ana and Ivan, had applied for them; and that my father's daughter and her husband, who were making application for her parents, were also named Ana and Ivan. "You can see how confusing this is," father said, "but the other Janko Bosiljevac isn't me. I am still here."

My childhood friends included my neighbor Drago Bosiljevac, who also was my second cousin. His grandpa, Janko Jarmek and my grandma, Ana (Jarmek) Bosiljevac, were brother and sister. Drago and I walked to school together, we played together in the dust, and we walked together to dances when we grew up. I remember many occasions when we played, but one sticks in my mind the most.

Once when Drago and I were eight years old, we took with us my brother Jure and our little neighbor, Mirko Hadusek, to have a little fun picking hazelnuts and blackberries. When we finished, it was too early to go home, so Drago and I decided to expand our adventure clear down to our former aristocratic family's yard, where all of Grice's children went whenever they had the opportunity. We call that place "Dvor Castle." When aristocrats lived there, they planted different kinds of fruit in their large yard. Apples, pears and plums were still there, many years after the owners left.

One particular apple tree bore fruit much earlier than any other in Grice, so that was the place we wanted to visit, although we were more interested in adventure then in something to eat. We arrived there, about 100 feet from Saint Ana's Chapel, where the apple tree stood in a small dip. We looked at the top of the tree, where the apples seemed the best – large and red. We threw sticks to get one down, but it took lots of sticks. Naturally, we were also knocking down other apples which we didn't want.

(St. Ana's Chapel and the area of that apple tree)

The yard's owners lived far away, but a family named Zeleznjak, who lived just across the valley, had the job of watching that property. When young Drago Zeleznjak showed up, we had no time to take any of the apples lying on the ground. The two younger children ran to a nearby cornfield, and Drago Bosiljevac and I thought to return for them as soon as Drago Zeleznjak left. After a while we came out of the bushes to take at least some pears which were sitting on the ground. As we bent down, we heard, "Oh, here you are!" If only we had been smarter we would have peeked out to see if he was gone, but it was too late for that. We two little brats just looked stunned when we spotted him right there under that pear tree. For us, the fun was over, but the punishment, unfortunately, was not. We just stood there saying nothing, thinking he would spank us and send us away. He didn't, but he wanted to have a little fun with us that wasn't what we would prefer.

Smiling, he ordered us to follow him to the damaged side of the apple tree. We followed like two frightened little puppies while he walked with long strides back to the tree. "Look what you have done," he said. "Now I want you to go to my mother in the house over there on that small hill and bring back a basket in which you will put these apples." That was worse than we had imagined. We would rather be spanked than to meet his mother, and we were certainly more afraid of her than we were of him.

(St. Ana's Chapel front)

As we walked from Saint Ana's Chapel down the hill toward my family's property which was right by his house, we planned to escape from that burden and run home. We thought he would see us, but my friend Drago had some idea on his own. A lady relative of his lived by that little forest close to my family's property and by that little house Zeleznjak lived in. We ran and arrived at Mara Novosel's home, and she seemed really happy to see us, offering us some cookies. We were being pretty quiet, so she asked Drago if his family had sent him with a message for her. He said, "No, we were just in the area so we decided to pay you a visit."

We left soon, planning to return home, but when we walked through that small forest onto the main road, we ran into the very person we were running from. Drago Zeleznjak had gone to his home to bring us that basket. For the second time he said, "Oh, here you are! Now, the two of you will follow me back to the apple tree."

Again we dragged along behind him, expecting the worst. He ordered us to pick up all of those apples lying on the ground. "What now?" we wondered. We were completely surprised when he said, "Now you two little kids take as many apples as you wish before you leave for home." We took only that one beautiful big apple which we had been after in the first place. Our exploring day was over. It had ended up being far more adventurous than we ever dreamed it would, and the two of us had learned our lesson.

As Drago and I grew up together, we had no idea that we both would one day be in America. Because his mother Ana was born in the USA, Drago and his entire family were able to immigrate easily to Pittsburg, Pennsylvania, where they settled during the 1960's. He and his wife Maxine now have two sons and two daughters. I have had the chance to visit with Drago and his family four times since we came to America.

These were some of the stories I remember about the people at Bosiljevac house No. 2 on our small Brdo.

Since house No. 3 was demolished before I was born, I don't have any memories of that family. The old people died, and the young went away, some to cities in Croatia and some to America, but their last name was, of course, Bosiljevac. After WWII, a man named Juro Bosiljevac appeared and started to build a small house on that property. We children asked our father who he was. He replied, "He is one member of the family who used to live there." While he worked on that house, he spoke with nobody in the neighborhood. We could tell he wasn't a friendly person at all. But little by little my father got acquainted with him, so when the house was finished and he moved in, he was invited to visit us. He came early in the evening when we had just lit those small petroleum lamps right after dinner. We were sitting by the warm stove during that winter, but we children sat somewhat away from the grownups to let them have their conversation, which was mostly about politics.

I remembered how much I loved to hear and learn about the world outside of Grice. Juro appeared to be an interesting person. He knew things from all over the world because he had been in many countries before returning home. It wasn't home at all without a house on his property, so he built one. He really had come to see a lady he had known before he left, but from then on he lived alone. The most interesting trip he spoke about was the one in which he hid out in the charcoal compartment of a ship on its way to America. He was found and sent back to Europe. He had a brother in America, but he never met him. Politics and the war were the only things that he and my father had in common.

The effort at friendship by my father was put aside because Juro was a rude person. He sued my father and others in the neighborhood for trespassing through his yard to get to our farm land, which had no other road to it. He lost the case because passing through the property on the edge of his yard was declared legal. After that, Juro had no friends on Brdo, except one lady who visited him, and he visited her occasionally. He died after I left, and the small house he had built was sold and taken away.

For some years, people would argue about one little piece of their land because nobody had enough of it. Our people told the story of one neighbor who moved a marking stone which designated the border between his and his neighbor's land so that he could have more land on which to plant his crop. When he died, area people heard his soul carrying that stone and crying "Where should I put it?" For a long time local people heard that, but once someone who hadn't known him when he was alive passed that way, and he also heard him. So, when the soul said, "Where should I put it?" the man said, "Put it wherefrom you took it." That apparently saved the man's soul, and it has been peaceful since.

My father and I talked about how some people chipped away a small piece of land, enlarging theirs by only a few inches. That was greedy, but the people were also truly needy. Life over there became too hard. That was a reason for all of us to leave. That era is gone. None of the farmers would be able to recognize their land borders, but nobody cares now. Today there is plenty of land there, but nobody who can work on it.

In house No. 4, another Juro Bosiljevac was born. He got married, had one daughter, and moved to Kansas City with his brother Ivan, a single man. Juro not only "forgot" that he had a family in Croatia, but he and Ivan also "forgot" that they had borrowed money from Janko Bosiljevac in house No. 1. Eventually, Juro had to give Janko the best piece of land he possessed because he had never repaid the money for that trip.

Juro's wife and child were suffering just like many others in the same situation. Roza's marriage to Peter Hrastovcak in the 1920's broke a perfect record of all residents having Bosiljevac surnames. They had three sons and a daughter named Ana. Ana was six years older than I, but when I became older she often took me with her to visit other girls. She was also my teacher, gradually pulling me out of my shell of teenage shyness.

51

The youngest son, Miho, settled in Australia, and the other two sons worked in Germany until their retirement.

The four settlements in upper Grice plus Novosel's Valley and Car's Valley down in lower Grice had about seventy families when I lived there. Now, however, many homes are abandoned. During the second half of the twentieth century, person after person was leaving until small Brdo and some of the other areas of our village were empty.

Turning from Brdo, it is about a ten-minute walk to Jarmek Valley. At one time in our history, every family there had the surname Jarmek. When I lived in Grice, five Jarmek families were living there, plus one family named Horvat. My grandmother was born in that place and so was my husband. Few of the Jarmeks, however, immigrated to Kansas City. Another ten-minute walk takes the traveler to Secen Valley. Some Secens still live in Kansas City. Fabac's Little Mountain, another ten-minute walk, is the highest point in Grice. Those people had a chestnut forest just up a sharp hill from their houses. Some Fabac families also live now in Kansas City.

Our village wasn't the only place known by such a name. Croatia's capital city, Zagreb, has a small hill named Grice in the center of the city. As far as I know, nobody has researched Grice's history, but there could be a connection with that name in Zagreb. Those imperialists who settled in our area may have come from Zagreb. It might be that they came from Zagorje, which is close to Zagreb, since we speak somewhat like the people from that area.

I remember when our Grice was full of people with their cattle, pigs, chickens, sheep, dogs and cats. In my mind I see even more clearly the children who played together. Some of us married there, and some left still single. We scattered over four continents, seeing each other rarely, some of us never meeting again. Emigration from Croatia has meant that even close family meetings have sometimes occurred on rare occasions. We are living more comfortable lives, of course, because we have left our poverty behind. From another point of view, however, we have lost the closeness of family, close friends, mutual histories and culture. Even visits in other countries with old friends show that we are now different people -- our looks have changed, and we have adapted to the new culture where we live.

(My childhood friend, Drago Bosiljevac, with his wife Maxine and a child)

People often like to forget those places in which they had such hard lives, but they should not. Some of those memories are wonderful. My own memories of Grice and the families who settled there will remain in my heart forever.

St. Ana Chapel

(See page 47)

(This is the new St. Ana chapel, built on land donated by Ana [Vidervoljd] Zeleznjak, who now lives in Hamilton, Canada.)

Chapter 3: **The Seasons of Our Lives**

One cold March day in 1939, all of us in my mother's family gathered to have <u>our picture taken</u>! This was very unusual; few of us had ever been photographed before, and no one in Golivrh even owned a camera. Grandmother's kind hearted brother, Matte Brozenic, was responsible for this special event.

(My grandparents Jagas and their four daughters and son Stjepan standing back on right. My mother on left, father, Drago and I in the white dress. Sister Bara on right with husband Miho, and their daughter Zdenka sitting on grandma's lap. Second row: Dragica on left of husband Miho. Middle: Milka, single.)

Matte had immigrated to Pittsburg when he was a young man, and his twin sister was in America, too. But he also loved another sister, my grandmother, Magdalena (Brozenic) Jagas, whom he had not seen since he left Croatia. Because of his love for her and their family, he hired a photographer and arranged for him to take the pictures. My mother and her sisters were scattered around, so getting us together wasn't so simple. In that area there was neither telephone nor transportation, but finally the big occasion was arranged. Since I was just three years old, I remember only that somebody spread a blanket behind the group outside their house. My mother had made a new dress for me, so although the day was very cold, she wouldn't let me wear even a sweater over it.

Grandfather Bosiljevac had been making us practice how we must pose to be in a picture. Many times he would entertain us by pretending to have a camera and taking our picture. "Stand still and put your hands straight down," he would caution us, then hitting himself on his behind and extending his hand toward us, he would promise, "Good. Come get your picture tomorrow." We children were delighted when he entertained us with this, and how he enjoyed making us laugh. That was the first picture ever taken of me, and we were lucky to have that one. Many folks never had their pictures taken when they were little. This was also my mother's first photograph, and she already had four children at the time.

A tiny child with light hair, I was known in our neighborhood as being quiet, sensitive and good natured. People probably liked me also because we had no other little girls on Brdo -- just plenty of boys. I must have seemed almost like a novelty in our small community.

When I was old enough to understand what responsibility means, I became obedient and took my duties seriously. My first one was to watch my little brother Jure, who was three years younger than I. When I was six or seven, someone usually watched me, but occasionally I was left at home when my parents and grandparents were out working on our farm. They weren't too far away, but still they trusted me to stay with Jure. Sometimes I took him by the hand and walked to where our parents were working. I wanted them to know that we were fine. They said I behaved just like a grown up person. Sometimes, my foxy little brother would say, "I can't walk up that hill." Then I would load him on my back and carry him. Our parents said I shouldn't because he was heavier than I, but I would reply, "When Jure doesn't want to walk, I have to."

Jure and I spent lots of time in our beautiful yard, wandering around or planting our own crop when there was nothing else to do. I enjoyed being as busy as a little bee most of the time. Either my parents asked me to do something or I found a job of my own to do. Although I did have a few dolls, we didn't play with toys. We didn't know what they were. My mother had taught me to be a responsible person. Even today, when I see something that needs doing, I do it rather than tell other members of my family to do it. That might not be all to the good: Perhaps I didn't teach my children to take responsibility as my mother had taught me to do.

During the winter on Brdo, when we were cooped up in the house, I would sneak out and walk across the road to the deserted house that Grandpa Tomo had built. We were using it only for storage of things like old clothes. I liked to make clothes for my dolls with them. The old chest in which these things were stored was all the furniture Grandma brought when she married Grandpa. *(Forty years later, when I got married, things were very different. My parents had a difficult time until they were able to prepare furniture for me to bring to my husband's family home where we would live.)*

We children helped our parents make sweaters, socks and mittens out of wool from our own sheep. Some of our clothes we made from hemp fiber, and for that the women first went through a long process to make the hemp into fabric.

No one in our village was rich, although some had more cropland than others. If a neighbor was short of food, he would help those with larger farms in exchange for food. All of us had just enough to survive. It still makes me sad to see those who suffer hunger and are without shelter. I never wished to be rich, but I do like to aid those who are suffering. I am pleased to be able to help others in a small way now.

Our priest here in Kansas City gave a sermon one Sunday in which he said, "You know a child, before he is able to talk, doesn't know but one thing – to pool everything toward his own little body. That is how selfish people are throughout their lives." I remember how when the communists replaced the aristocratic system in Croatia. They said, "We all have to be equal, no wealthy or poor." When I lived in Yugoslavia under their system, I heard some say, "Well, at least the communists succeeded with one half of their philosophy – they abolished wealth, but not poverty." Selfishness will never fade away. Communism didn't work either. It just created another system in which all those who were in their party lived well, and those who were not couldn't get ahead even if they worked hard. The communists were aware of every person who had a bit more money, so they imposed taxes on them.

Most of the world's people live today in large cities where outdoor activities are limited. When I lived in the countryside, we had to create our own play outside. Children today have lots and lots of toys with which they quickly get bored, but we never were. Constantly we could find something interesting to do in our open areas. The world today is changing, but I wish we could keep an appreciation of things like a clean and healthy environment.

Ribnik County had very little crime except for the time during the war or when communists punished those who were against their regime. The only stealing I remember involved an occasional vegetable. Once a man in Grice stole some hay to feed his horses, and his neighbor sued him in court. The wife of the accused had never been to court before, or any place away from home, but she was called as a witness. Neighbor ladies had advised her not to admit anything, but when the judge asked her, "Did your husband bring home stolen property?" she answered, "He did, but I don't want to admit it." The judge began to laugh, and so did everybody else in court.

Of course, not everyone in our area was an angel. We had people who liked to be malicious, but they knew life for them would be impossible without the other people in the community. We needed each other, and we needed our children to marry locally if possible, but nobody would marry a person if his or her family had done something bad. Our hard lives made us stronger, more responsible people. I strongly believe that was the main reason for the small amount of crime. Another was because we lived in a place where everybody knew everybody. Being poor doesn't make people steal, but it might make one who grew up without learning how to work, or somebody whose parents hadn't taught the person honesty more susceptible.

Mother's sewing machine always fascinated me. When I was still small, she wouldn't let me touch it, but how I wanted to learn to sew! When mother went to Karlovac one time, I tried to take that machine apart, even though I was forbidden to use it. Once I stuck the machine needle clear through my nail, learning the hard way why mother had made that rule. Even that didn't stop me, however. I continued to beg, and Mom finally let me learn how to use it properly. I never had any training in tailoring, but I did learn to sew for myself and some of my friends. Eventually, this experience helped me to get my first job when I came to America. Our parents couldn't afford to give us children more than four years of grade school education. That was all that was available in our local area. At least we did learn how to read and write and understand some of our Croatian history before the communists took over. After that I still took two years more of school, but we had to learn only what they taught, like their songs and war.

I understood why we could get no further education, but all of the political and social changes that we lived through did give me more of an understanding of our own Croatian history, which I now am able to share with others. Our descendants need to understand what conditions drove us from our homes. For example, when a family had a son, he inherited his father's small farm. When there were two or more sons, however, the property had to be split among them, making their small farmland even smaller.

Another type of difficulty could also quickly ruin a family's future – fire. In 1940, when I was only five years old, this giant thing happened in our neighborhood. We children slept with our grandparents in the main house, but our parents slept across the road in our spare house. Petar Hrastovcak banged on their door that night, shouting, "Janko, it's Petar. Wake up and come help me. My house is burning!" My parents jumped up and ran to the main house to tell my grandparents. They sneaked out carefully so as not to wake us children. The burning house was about 600 feet from our house. Drago and I woke up to see giant flames through our windows. We dressed quickly to run to that burning home, leaving little Jure in his crib. My father stood on top of a structure twenty feet from the fire, throwing water on the roof. Nobody was throwing water on the burning house itself, but rather on other structures close to it. Luck was on our side since the weather was calm and there was water in our ponds. Our grandfather had taught us some English words, and one of them was "fire." My grandma took that opportunity and went to the edge of the Brdo yelling "Fire, Fire!" as loudly as she could, while facing down to Novosel Valley and Car's Valley. Thanks to Grandpa, everybody knew what that meant.

All eight homes on Brdo were wood houses covered with straw. Malca Bosiljevac, whose husband Juro had gone to Kansas City, now became even poorer than before. Evidently, she had forgotten to secure a flame when she boiled water to wash her clothes. She and seven other family members were living in her house, a house she lost that night.

When house No. 4 burned down, that family needed to replace it, but how? Of course, everyone in our community was willing to help. Malca was fortunate that house No. 5, my family's original home, was vacant. It was owned by my grandfather's cousin Josip and his wife. Josip had died long before, and his widow Ana had moved to her daughter's when Mildred emigrated to Kansas City with her family. Ana gave her house in Grice to Malca rent-free as long as she needed it. After Malca's family moved in, we children visited them and finally got to see the inside of the house where our grandpa was born.

Two years later Hrastovcaks bought a wooden house and relocated it to their property. When they built that house in 1942, it created plenty of excitement for us neighborhood children. We had never seen a house being built. When carpenters came to work in the morning, a house was already up in the air, so we ran to see and jumped up to the second floor. Father soon called Jure and me to come eat breakfast before the adults had to leave to farm. At first I ignored him. He called again, and we reluctantly came home, but it was too late for us. My father was usually calm, but I discovered then that he did indeed have a temper. That was the only time he spanked me. It wasn't needed again. We had learned that if we obeyed him, all of us would be happier.

Drago, however, was an ignorant boy who never paid much attention to what somebody was telling him. He knew about father's temper, but he went his own way, visiting friends and staying with them for a very long time. Sometimes father would get hysterical when he tried to turn Drago around, but it doesn't usually work with a personality like Drago's. He just wanted to be with his friends all the time, even hanging around with older boys. Sometimes they could chase him away; then he would come home crying. Our parents advised him to stay away from older kids, but Grandma didn't stop there. She found those older boys and argued with them, calling them names and defending her grandson. It was true that Drago was a lovable child, and older people liked him because of his personality.

Jure was completely different. The two didn't even look like brothers. Like our father, Jure was strong in character, even with the same temper, but he looked more like Mother with blue eyes and blond hair. Drago resembled Father's family, brown hair and hazel eyes. I was different than any of them, light brown hair and green eyes, with less temper than Father and more courage than Mother.

Jure waited impatiently to grow up so he could make his own decisions. Father was right to give us advice and manners when we were young, but Jure didn't like that. He left home right after he came home from military service and soon was driving a bus in Ljubljana, Slovenia, but that didn't last too long. Even in a communist country, Jure managed to develop his own business. He bought a truck first and worked with that. Later he bought machines in Germany and made frames for eyeglasses. When his son Marko finished school as an optician, he opened his own space, so there were two optical companies where Jure and Marko worked.

As children, however, we found our pleasures outside when winter finally lost its harsh grip on Grice. Nature awakened our spirits with its beauty. Our yard was what we enjoyed the most, and our attached property which stretched far away, clear to the forest. From our place farther up, fern fields dotted with many birch trees covered the entire hill with lovely light green leaves. We used fern for the cattle's beds in our stable, and birch wood to start a fire in the stove. To start the fire easily, our men sliced thin slices of wood and dried them. Sometimes children would bring cattle to graze on those fields, but when people had time for pleasure, they strolled on that hill, taking in the panoramic view far away from our village.

The month of May was a heavenly time for all of us, adults and children alike. Everything suddenly came to life before our eyes. Father liked to plant different kinds of fruit trees in our yard. When they began to bloom, our yard filled with fragrance. Later, when the fruit had ripened, we had plenty to eat, especially apples and walnuts, through the summer and far into the winter. Mulberries were first to bloom, and since no one had them except us, they attracted the whole neighborhood. We let friends take as many as they wanted. Cherries offered another taste treat early in the summer. We also had at least three varieties of plums. When it was a good year for them, we made sljivovica (plum whiskey). Sales of this provided us with a rare source of cash money. The last fruit, harvested during the fall, included apples, walnuts, hazelnuts and chestnuts. These were plentiful and provided another source of the income which we desperately needed.

Nature woke up in the spring, and we did, too. Under the blue May sky we would walk through a shady and fragrant paradise when those fruit trees began to bloom. Under their blossoms luscious green grass showed off its decorations, small flowers of many kinds which emerged from the ground, awakened by the April rains. Now the warm sun and southern breezes caressed them.

For much of the year there was little joy in our daily lives, but the overpowering beauty and fragrance of spring helped heal our spirits each year. I often lay on the ground looking up to the blooming fruit trees and watched how the sun seeped through those leaves and flowers. It felt as if I were hiding away from something. Unless one has actually been there, it is hard to describe. I loved that gentle flickering of lush grass and the fragrance in the air. The nature I loved is one I could touch, hear, smell and see. All of my senses were caressed in our own yard and down by our sparkling spring, gushing clean was for us to drink and wash our clothes. Then Mother and I brought home freshly washed laundry and hung it up in our yard where it absorbed the fragrant air, flicked by south breezes. It was wonderful to touch it, smell it and look at it before storing it away in our drawers.

In Europe, May first is a national holiday; therefore, we children loved to decorate our homes for that occasion. Jure and I cut up small birch trees, bringing them home to decorate our porch. Our neighbors to the west did the same. They cut two tall birches, tied them on each side of the road by their home, and brought the tops together so neighbors could walk under that giant arch-. Birch trees refuse to grow tall. Maybe that explains their delicate beauty.

Another joy in spring was the birds returning from the south, ready to build the nests in which their babies would enter the world in just three weeks. We children competed to discover who could find the most nests. The birds brought real joy to us, but not that much to the adults who had to deal with birds feeding themselves with our crops. We had both big and very small birds, flitting around in all kinds of colors. I thought Croatia must have every type of bird in the world.

My brothers and I also competed regarding who could climb the highest tree. I never let my brothers leave me behind in any competition. Constantly I wanted to do whatever they did, climbing, running, lifting weights and even working. Mother wanted to teach me to work with her, but I preferred to do things with the boys, who were young and full of energy. After I came to America, it came in handy that I knew how to cut grass and pound nails into a piece of wood. When Drago left home, I worked with my father doing different types of chores. That made me feel happy and important, and I later continued to help my husband wherever I was needed.

The spring was wonderful, with time to play and enjoy nature, but there was also hard work to be done. Even as small as we were, we had to help our parents prepare crops on which we depended for survival. As summer came, we worked in the hot sun all day long, and we children were plenty tired in the evening. But our parents had been out as long as we had. When we came home, mother would cook dinner for all of us while father cared for the cattle. When our friends came, however, we all ran out to play games outside. Mother often wondered how we could run and play after working all day long. We were tired, of course, but not tired enough to refuse games with our friends.

All of our crops were planted by hand. We used no mechanical instruments other than the plow which our oxen pulled. So, during the summer we had no rest except when it rained. That may be the reason I still enjoy the rain. When summer was rainy we were fine, but when summers were dry, like 1950 and 1951, my father and I went to get water from Obrh Creek. One of those years, we had to go with our oxen 19 times, just like Father had done in 1935.

During the war, there wasn't any government assistance whatsoever; we were lucky if the government didn't tax us heavily on our land, the only source of our survival. Our homegrown food was the only food we had during the war and after, even until I left Croatia in 1957. Doctors now tell us we must eat vegetables and fruit. That was what we grew and ate then, very little meat. If we had some meat it would be pork or chicken. We ate mostly whole wheat bread, no cookies or pies, no cakes or candy. Until I grew up, I never ate anything sweet.

Rarely we children had nothing to do during harvest time. Once, however, when I was still little, some friends and I decided to stroll away from Brdo. The neighbor kids told us, "Come on. We can get some corn at Janko Jarmek's corn field." At that young age, my brother and I didn't know that was wrong. When we brought the ears home, we gave them to Grandma to cook for us. She wasn't as honest as my parents, so she agreed. Luckily, she hadn't cooked it before my parents came home. Father saw that corn and asked us where we had gotten it. We told him it was from Janko Jarmek's field. We thought nothing was wrong with that, but it was plenty wrong to my father. He said, "Right this moment you take this back to Janko Jarmek's house and give it to him. At the same time, you will apologize." Of course, the worst part was to have to go to his house and get embarrassed. We asked Mother if we could take the ears and throw them into Janko Jarmek's field. Mother was more understanding of our feelings, and she said, "Yes, that is good enough." So, my brother Drago took it, but on his way he stopped at his friends' house to ask if they were taking their corn back. "No," they replied, "Our grandma already cooked it and we ate it." I'm glad my parents taught us that kind of honesty because it has really stuck in our minds forever.

The values our mother gave us were different because she was a religious person. She constantly told us rules for behavior from her prayer book: "Don't steal. Don't do anything wrong to others even if somebody does wrong to you. Don't take revenge. God will take care of the situation without you. Be happy with what you have and don't wish to have what others have." That was the best advice I ever received. Father wasn't as religious as mother, but he gave us the same advice, although it sounded different, something like this: "Don't hurt anybody's feelings. Don't take anything that belongs to someone else. Be nice to people. Don't come home if you do something wrong to someone." We never left home before he repeated those things. Well, it pays to have had the kind of parents we had.

Fall was beautiful, with leaves falling to the ground and most of our crops ready for harvesting. We children loved the fall when families decided to harvest grapes. Usually our whole neighborhood did this at the same time. Some of our neighbors had relatives who lived far away. They rarely came for a visit, but they did come to help pick grapes, giving us a chance to see them and their children. Everybody in Ribnik County had a vineyard. Some families had enough only for themselves, but others had more than they could use, so they sold some. Our family had one parcel at a distant location, and when it was time to pick the grapes we went along for the fun of being with other people and their children.

No matter what type of food it was, Mother was happiest when we brought the harvest home. Then she would say, "We have to be thankful to God, who helped us have enough food for the entire year." We didn't celebrate Thanksgiving over there, but my mother had expressed it best.

As fall drew to a close, I counted how many more projects we had to complete before winter. It seemed to me we would never complete our work before snow would cover the ground. But the snow would bring a good rest for us after that long, hard summer. Those men who had been working in America gladly returned home to rejoin their families, be their own bosses, and get some hard earned rest.

In the early 1940's, our winters were harsh and long. Heavy snow lay on the ground from November to March. There wasn't much outdoor work for adults to do, but we children had to go to school, plodding in heavy snow though we were poorly dressed. Our feet and small bodies were always miserably cold.

The ladies kept busy knitting sweaters, socks and mittens, and prepared threads to make the fabric they would later use for sheets, tablecloths and even some boys' pants. (This fabric would later have to be dyed.) The men's job was to feed their cattle and cut wood to warm their homes.

There was, of course, no radio or television to give us weather forecasts, but Grandma usually predicted when snow would come. She would say, "Birds are flying under the roof; snow is coming." Or, "Everything smells like snow today, so we can expect it soon." She didn't really mean that snow smelled, but rather that there was a dense overcast which left a close feeling in the air. She had many funny phrases, some of which she heard from other people and some she made up by herself. She was often amusing and a good step-grandma to us children.

Sometimes heavy snow fell overnight so that the branches of our fruit trees hung to the ground. The first child to awake to this called everybody in the house to enjoy the excitement. Unless it was a school day, we could hardly wait to dress and get outside. We told the family we were going to shake snow down from the fruit trees. That was our excuse, but really we wanted to go play in the snow. The family didn't want us to get cold and wet, but it didn't bother us at all to come back in the house as icicles.

Once I remember getting on our sled right by the house, facing down to a little valley. I asked Jure to get on with me to go down the hill together. I didn't really mean to go down myself. I just pretended I wanted to. Luckily Jure refused to get on because soon, since my short legs couldn't reach the ground, my sled took off, and I found myself on the way down into that quite steep valley. I was afraid of hitting a large tree or a rock, but I was slightly luckier to hit only a small pear tree. There were other times when we did get hurt.

We constantly hoped to catch some of those colorful blue jays. We prepared a trap with corn in it. Finally my brother and I were lucky to get one blue jay. We brought it into our house and kept it for a little while. We let it go when we became aware how unhappy that adorable bird was in our hands.

Christmas was a happy time for us, even though we had no presents for anyone in the family. This was normal since we never heard that anyone over there received presents. Our celebration began on Christmas Eve when Mother decorated a corner of our table. There she hung four pictures of saints that she had decorated with raffia. We didn't have Christmas trees because in our area, evergreens didn't grow. Preparations on Christmas Eve included a centerpiece for the table and a special bread which I still make every Christmas for my family. When the grandparents were alive, Grandma baked that bread, then decorated the table with bread in the middle, with candles, a rosary and keys from the basement by it. There were some other things which I have forgotten. Hay was put under the tablecloth and under the table. It was Grandpa's job to bring in the hay. When the lamps were lit, we children lay under the table on the hay, just as Jesus did. That was a special treat for us.   The other was when our grandfather brought homemade wine from the basement and gave each child a sip of it from a special claylike pitcher.

As Christmas Eve was a fast day in the Catholic religion, we could not have eaten meat (but we didn't have any to spare, anyway). After Grandma died, Mother always had a special meal, cheese strudel and other things made of cheese and vegetables. We children were free to visit our friends to see how their mothers had decorated their houses, then they came to see our decoration. We had to be home by midnight to eat the special meat which Grandpa baked. We were then free to go to bed, but to honor Jesus' birth, the rest of the family didn't sleep the entire night. Christmas morning we ate breakfast and got ready for church. Through the usually heavy snow, it was at least a one-hour walk there and another one back. When we returned, all tired and hungry, a table full of food was waiting for us. There would be a turkey or goose or some kind of pork, or maybe just a large chicken with chicken soup. Mother also baked bread and some pastry, and potato salad and homemade sausages. What a special day for us to enjoy delicious food in quantities not usual for us. Our candles were lit on Christmas evening and burned until midnight. Our decorations stayed up until January 6th, celebrating the day the three wise men arrived to see baby Jesus. After that, our holiday was over.

When I was growing up, our winters were long and hard, and everybody got tired of that weather. Usually, by Valentine's Day the southern breezes were on the way to melt our stubborn snow, and by Palm Week, the fruit trees were on their way to bloom.

Other springs, other summers and falls of hard work followed by winters of cold and snow kept arriving, until our villagers disappeared one by one. Only those who had no place to go or were too old to leave remained. Grice's pasture still waits for cattle to cut its grasses and clean the meadows, but they also have disappeared. Birds fly in looking for fields full of wheat but cannot find it, so some of them have gone, as well. Ribnik County is now a sad place: no more young people who sing as they return home from church or dance hall. Once Easter was a happy day when we walked from our church singing so that people far away could hear us, but now everything there has ended, so the singing has ended, too.

Chapter 4: **Families of Golivrh** *(Barepeak)*

Golivrh, the village in which my mother was born, is in Ribnik County, Lipnik parish. As Grice is the first village on the left side of the highway going from Karlovac, so Golivrh is on the right, but farther away from the highway. Its name probably came from its appearance, as it was up on a high peak without large trees. Only smaller fruit trees grow there. When people settled there, fruit trees didn't exist; the hill was bare.

Golivrh was comprised of two sections, Lower and Upper Golivrh. My grandparents, Marko and Magdalena Jagas, lived on the edge of Lower Golivrh, as did most families with the surname Jagas. Other families there included Bravaric, Svazic and Listar. Most of these people immigrated to Kitchener, Canada, including my cousin, Ana Drgastin, with her husband Ivan and their daughter Nedeljka. Later they were able to bring my aunt, Ana's mother, Dragica Maver.

People living on Golivrh had good land without any rocks in it, but their disadvantages were a road that was very muddy when it rained and their distance from our highway. From Brdo we were able to see the house where my grandparents lived, but without telephones we couldn't talk to them unless we walked about four miles to their home.

When they needed each other, people whose villages were close to those of their relatives were better off; those who married people from distant villages had to send their children on foot to contact relatives. My brother Drago and I were messengers whenever our parents needed to send a message or deliver something to Golivrh. Even if our grandparents were not home when we got there, we knew they were on their scattered fields, not far away.

The view in Upper Golivrh was incredible! When I was there I thought I was on top of the world, seeing all four sides far away laid out as an immense panorama. One side of Upper Golivrh *(toward the Netretic where people got to the highway and to Karlovac)* had a level surface. That didn't obstruct the view of elevated mountains in the distance. From Upper Golivrh we could see almost the entire county of Ribnik and beyond it.

When Drago and I went to our grandparents' home, mother would remind us not to wait till close to sunset before we started home. If we did, we would be walking home in darkness. In Grice, daylight lingered long after sunset, but not in Golivrh. We had to be certain we were not traveling through that thick forest in darkness unless an older person was walking with us.

During the dry season it wasn't so hard to go there, even if we had to walk through thick forest; but when it rained, that was another story: First we traveled down by our Saint Ana Chapel, then about one-fourth of a mile to cross the highway, then down to a creek which was hard to cross. In the really wet season it wasn't easy to find dry surfaces anywhere in that valley. Sometimes it seemed to us that water was bubbling out everywhere. Past that hurdle, we encountered an area in which people had previously cut out forest. Then, ten years later, young trees and bushes had grown so thick that we could see only the little path we were walking on. I'll admit that I was afraid of the wicked wolf. Nobody had actually seen any wolves there for many years, but we had heard stories about them and imagined they were still in the forest. Proceeding through and climbing up a hill and down again, we reached another creek. That one was a real pain to cross. There was no bridge of any kind, so we would keep looking for a better spot. Sometimes we succeeded, but other times we arrived at our grandparents' home with wet shoes.

On one occasion Grandfather Marko, who was working in his yard, spotted us before Grandma did. With a happy smile he welcomed us. As Grandma was a short distance away, he said, "I will play a joke on Grandma. You two just stay here and say nothing till I finish." As he loved to joke with people, Grandma already knew him well, so he had a hard time succeeding with his joke on her, but he tried. "Magda," he said, look! Our neighbor's kids have come to visit us." Magda couldn't see well at her age, so she walked closer to be certain who we really were before speaking. He hadn't fooled her. When she recognized us she smiled and said, "Oh, no, you don't fool me. These are our grandchildren from Grice, Drago and Ana."

(Left: Marko and Magdalena Jagas.)

When Grandma Magdalena married Grandpa, she had come from the Brozenic family, who lived a short distance away on the edge of Upper Golivrh. Grandma had nobody from her family visiting when I came there because her twin brother, Matt Brozenic, and their sister had immigrated to Pittsburg. Leaving their farm, he and his wife Dorty let her niece live there with her family, and he left Matt's property to her. She married Mato Jarnevic, grandson of Josip Bosiljevac, the oldest brother of my grandfather Tomo Bosiljevac. Josip became a victim of an old Croatian law when he married his wife, who had the last name of Jarnevic. Since he came to live in her family's home, he had to take his wife's last name, and, of course, their children also had to be known by their mother's surname. We were related on my Bosiljevac side, so it would be nice if we had the same name.

(Of course, if that law had been in effect when my great-great grandfather married, all of us descendants would have been surnamed Car [Zcar], not Bosiljevac! Most of the other families in Upper Golivrh were surnamed Svazic. Many later settled in Kitchener, Canada, and some in Kansas City, as well.)

Next to Golivrh is a village named Gorice (Little Mountain). Families who settled there were named Drgastin, Plavan, Zupetic, Pestak and Brozenic. All of these surnames are now represented in Kansas City, as well as in other places. Although Golivrh and Gorice are close to each other, residents could not talk to one another without walking down into the deep valley between them.

Without telephones, communication was difficult. We never dreamed that phones, as well as piped water and electricity, would ever be possible. Perhaps the emigrations from such villages would not have been as frequent had such "luxuries" been available. Our foreign occupiers hadn't paid much attention to the local people's quality of life. Instead, they developed elegant areas for the rich, such as the Adriatic Coast (our main tourist region) and Slavonia, which was wealthy in its agriculture. The only "quality" we had came from our clean, pure air and water, the beauty of our forests, mountains and springs, as well as our spectacular views.

The third village on the right side of the highway was Stranica. Most of its residents shared the surname Cavlovic. On the little peak above the village sits the Chapel of St. Peter, which is almost large enough to be called a church. From Grice, as well as from many other villages, we could see that lovely chapel. Next to the chapel is a cemetery belonging to those villages on the right side of the highway. My grandparents Jagas are buried there with a family monument installed by my great uncle, Matt Brozenic.

(At the monument: four daughters, my father, and Milka's husband Ivan.)

From the Lipnik forest, when the trees are bare in winter, St. Peter's Chapel looks so close that it seems one could reach it with an outstretched hand, since it sits at the same height. The physical trip between, however, would involve going down to the highway and then up again to the chapel.

Beyond that hill was another village called Novaki, home to families named Zeleznjak, Dolinar, Gojmerac and Zugecic.

I never had the opportunity to visit the other village in our area. It was on still higher elevation than any I have mentioned. This village was named Mrtinski Vrh (Peak). We could see it from many places, and I am certain those villagers could see wide open areas all around their homes. I can remember only two surnames among its people – Ratkaj and Cigic.

These, then, were the villages of Golivrh, the area in which my grandparents Jagas lived. Their marriage and their efforts to improve life for their descendants (and, of course, war and politics) determined the course of their lives . . . and, eventually, of mine.

Like many of his countrymen, Grandpa Jagas went to America twice and returned home both times. He had married before he left, but had no children yet, so Grandma lived at home with her husband's parents. When he returned for good, the couple was ready to start their family, but they had no success until they sought professional help. It may have been witchery, but Grandma had their first child when she was twenty-eight, followed by eight more, including one set of twins who died right after birth.

Their first child, Marko, married when he was eighteen years old and his wife, Mara Drgestin, was only fifteen. A smart but arrogant young man, Marko had married to get the bride's price from her father in Canada. My father told me the story of my uncle Marko, who moved his wife in the house with his brothers and sisters. When the marriage money was almost gone, he and his father, also named Marko, thought about what to do. Grandpa was in the business of buying and selling cattle. He traveled to Karlovac every Friday to the cattle market. Being bright and somewhat foxy, Grandpa found a man during one trip who sold him a passport for his son Marko. So, just a few months after his marriage young Marko was on his way to Argentina. He shook off his financial difficulties there, but he had left a wife in the already crowded home.

My mother sometimes told me stories about herself and the other Mara, Marko's wife, saying, "We were like two sisters, sometimes going to dances together." My mother, who was older than her own sisters, was a year younger than Marko's wife.

Marko had emigrated to Argentina, as had other young men from the village, in 1928. During the Depression, none of these men ever returned, including Marko. Life in Argentina was hard for all immigrants, but for Marko, who was naturally smart, life was better. He educated himself, reading and writing in Spanish and English, therefore getting an office job with a company owned by Croatians. Like all of his family, Marko was good in math and was able to handle the company's accounting.

(Marko Jagas in Argentina)

For a few years after Marko left, his wife Mara stayed with his family. Marko exchanged letters with her and helped her with some money, but did not send for her. Mara was free of all obligation – no children, no home of her own, no property. So, what was the problem? No one in our family discussed the situation in front of us children, but I have my own theory about it: Marko had immigrated to Argentina using somebody else's passport, and he was known there by that person's name, so he wasn't able to get papers for his wife, who had his real surname, Jagas.

When Mara realized that her husband would not come home or bring her to Argentina, she had to look out for her own future. She went to Zegreb where she worked as a housekeeper, the only work a woman from the country could get during that time before World War II. During the war, communication was nonexistent, so she knew nothing about Marko. When the war was over, they did start to communicate again, and to everybody's surprise, he brought her at last to Argentina! How he managed the paper work was never discussed, but they were together again. By that time, it was late to start a family of their own, but Mara had brought to Argentina her niece, Ljubica Spudic, from Grice.

So, Marko and Mara's story had a happy ending, but this was, unfortunately, not true of others. The oldest child, son of Marko and Magda Jagas, left Croatia when he, too, was eighteen. Neither his parents nor his brothers or sisters ever saw him again, a sad situation for the entire family. Their second child, Anton, was born with a slight speech difficulty caused by an undergrown tongue. With little money and no health insurance, Anton never got medical help. He never married and died before he was sixty years old. The grandparents also had the pair of twins who died right after birth. A priest from our church said that babies have to be baptized before they die, and the twins looked very weak, so Grandpa and another family member walked through the night to have the babies baptized.

My mother, Mara, was the fourth child and the first girl born. She came into the world January 10, 1915. My mother's life, through stories she told me and her whole attitude, was one of sadness. She told of how her mother-in-law was mean and abusive to her, and said that the large family was always hungry because their father liked to drink more than he should. Grandfather Jagas, was not a good provider for his family, and, it was true, was frequently drunk, but he never hit his wife or children. When he returned from America, he bought more property and built new houses. This brought some prosperity, but later he turned around when he began dealing in the cattle market business. Perhaps the change was due to his drinking with customers.

Grandma almost died at one point in her life, and the doctor ordered her to do no heavy work for a long time. So, even the small children had to help. As the oldest of the four girls, my mother had to take care of many things with Grandma advising her. Mother told me she had never missed school, even though it was took one hour to walk there and another back, and that she was the best student in all of her classes. A teacher once wrote to her father, "Dear Mr. Jagas, come to school because we need to talk to you about your daughter Mara." Grandpa was very proud of his daughter's grades, so he was glad to meet the teacher. He got what he had expected, praise of Mara from her teacher, but something more. "Mara should continue her education," the teacher urged. But there was no way he could finance this. Higher education was available only farther from home, which would mean paying for her to live with somebody in the city in addition to the cost of the school.

Mother's chance was not the only one that was not typical. When Bara, the second oldest girl, was attending school, the teacher and her husband, also a teacher, saw that Bara wouldn't be going on for further education. They asked Grandpa if he would let her work for them there, where they lived by the school. Since Bara wasn't suited for farm work and he had other children at home, Grandpa let her go. The couple taught her to cook and do house work.

When she was old enough to get married, they introduced her to one of their relatives who was in the special police. His duty station was in Macedonia, so if they married, that would be where she would go to live. He made good money, but he wasn't near enough for them to meet, so they had only pictures of each other. Before he ever saw her in person, he showered her with gifts. Bara knew he was ten years older than she, but he looked nice in his uniform. Since she didn't wish to return to farm life, she agreed to be engaged to him. But when he finally came to meet her, Bara had second thoughts. Other men were interested in her, and she had a playful and happy nature, while he was a serious, mature man. On the other hand, none of the young farmers could give her as good a life as could Miho Savor, her fiancé. Her family wanted her to have a better life, so they urged her to not throw away this chance. So Bara and Miho were married and went to Macedonia.

At the beginning of their married life, Bara became very unhappy. They were far away from any cities in Macedonia, and people even talked differently there. Miho didn't know what to do with Bara, so he asked my father (the only person who could go there) to come talk with her. When he arrived, she told father how her husband worked long hours, leaving her alone, seeing nobody. She had no chance to go to a city, and the countryside looked just like Golivrh.

Both times she became pregnant and was nearing her time, she went to her parents' home to give birth. The first girl was Zdenka, a year younger then I; the second girl was named Ruzica. When World War II erupted in Yugoslavia, Miho came to Croatia to serve in the Croatian police in the Lika region. By that time, Bara and their two children were able to be with him.

During the last few years of the war, Miho served in the Croatian army. In 1945, they moved to Karlovac. Now the family consisted of four to feed, but how? Miho had been in the losing army, so neither he nor Bara had a job. By that time, communists were in power in Yugoslavia. Bara went to visit Mrkopalj, where she received food from some friends, but many had left; others were still alive but quiet, feeling lucky just to be alive still.

Soon after Bara arrived, however, the authorities arrested her and sent a telegram to her husband, stating that if he ever wanted to see Bara again he must come to exchange himself for his wife. People thought that the federal government was unaware of that arrest, that it was only local communists who saw this as a way to get rid of men who had served in the Croatian army.

My father met Miho in Karlovac and heard what had happened. Miho said, "Tell my family that I am going up there for the exchange – there is nothing else I can do." When he showed up, the communists released Bara and put Miho in jail. In the shortest time possible, they had some kind of communist-style hearing and gave Miho ten years jail time. They sent him to Karlovac to be with his family until he would be called. Not long after, they called him back to Mrkopalj. No one knows what happened then, but his wife got a telegram from the authorities which said, "You can come here to claim your husband's clothes." Fearing what they might do to her, Bara never went. Neither she nor his family ever knew what happened to him. Did they kill him? Or had he joined others who just disappeared following the war?

In 1992, the European Union recognized Croatia's independence. The new government discovered underground tunnels in that part of Croatia similar to those in Slovenia. The tunnels had been secret during the communist regime, so residents claim that some of those who disappeared had dug the tunnels secretly. After the prisoners finished digging, who knows what was done to them. Certainly my uncle Miho Savor's fate has never been known, which is a double pain for the family.

Bara was in Karlovac with her two daughters, without a job or any income. The new government wasn't sympathetic to a family whose husband and father served in the opposition army and who had been killed by the new government's loyalists. Bara never even attempted to seek help from the communists; if she had, they would have declined to help her anyway. So family from the countryside helped her a little with food, but that wasn't enough. One lady named Facanka, however, was full of immeasurable kindness. She owned a small restaurant in Rijecka Ulica, the street where Bara lived. I remember being in her restaurant when I was older. She gave my aunt a job as well as food to take home to her daughters. After some years Bara got a job in a factory named ZE-CE where she worked until her retirement. Wages were small, so she and her girls lived from one paycheck to another. Whenever any of her relatives were in that town they always stopped at Bara's apartment to bring some food for the family.

During school vacations, the daughters loved to come to grandparents Jagas and to us in Grice. We had a great time playing in our yard, especially the two girls who were eager to get in our open spaces and enjoy nature. Once when Zdenka spent a longer time with us, she knew my father was going to be in Karlovac for some shopping and would see her mother and sister. Zdenka asked him to bring a swim suit that her mother had promised her. As soon as father arrived home, she raced to claim her long awaited possession and slipped it on as soon as she got it. Because we country children were shy and conservative, we would never go out in a swim suit, but Zdenka could hardly wait to put it on and burst out of the house, running through our yard in it. My mother ran after her yelling, "Zdenka, this isn't Korana in Karlovac where you used to swim!" But she replied, "Aunt Mara, there is nothing wrong with it. Don't you know I don't have something new very often? I'm excited." So all of us laughed and hoped nobody saw her running through the yard.

When Zdenka finished high school, she met a young Serbian man who was divorced. During the communist era, Croatians and Serbians were getting married because religion didn't matter to them. Neither his divorced status nor his nationality would have mattered if he had been a good person, but he didn't have a job. All he had was good looks, which didn't bring happiness to anybody. They had no apartment of their own and had to live with Bara in her two-room apartment. Things were very difficult: Zdenka loved her mom and sister Ruzica to whom she had brought a real difficulty: Her husband didn't work, but he sometimes bought things on his wife's and mother-in-law's credit. Zdenka got very sick from pressure on her brain and was hospitalized. She survived, but before she returned home, her husband had left, and she never saw him again. Even after he was gone, he left some credit payments for them to pay off.

After Zdenka got well, she met a nice man who was in the army, and they planned to marry in the near future. But when she visited him one weekend on the Adriatic coast, she had a stroke again during the night and died at the age of 29. Zdenka was a person with a large, warm heart. She was never embarrassed with her older mother or any of us farm relatives. When she was with her friends who were better educated than we were, she would embrace and kiss us, even if we met in the center of Karlovac. "This is so-and-so in my family," she would explain fondly. When she died, I was already in America and far away from the sadness of her death.

Bara's younger daughter, Ruzica, also married a young Serbian. He was different than her sister's husband, although church didn't matter to them either during the communist era. The communists had great power over young people, especially in the cities, and poisoned their minds against religion. For many young folk, going to church became a shame, and many would not even have their children baptized. The communists told people: "You expect God to give you something, but the church doesn't give anything, it only takes your money."

Still, the marriage of Ruzica and Branko survived the Croatian and Serbian War during the nineties. I met Branko in 1986 when my family and I visited Croatia, and found that I liked his kindness. Aunt Bara, who had a hard life, died at the age of 74, before Croatia became an independent country.

The seventh child of grandparents Jagas, a son Stjepan, was born in 1918. I remember him only as a nice looking man. He married Bara Jarnevic two years before he volunteered in the partisan army which was on the side of the communists. Everybody was surprised when young men from Golivrh and Veselice volunteered for that army. Although my mother and the rest of his family objected to his decision, obviously that hadn't stopped him. Those young men thought the war would be over quickly, and they would get good positions in the communist party, but they were wrong. The war just started in our place, but it lasted another two years.

Stjepan's sister Milka, the youngest child, had married Stjepan's wife's brother Ivan, so Ivan also joined that army. The Jagas brothers and sisters were all smart, but they couldn't get a higher education where we lived. Stjepan believed he could at least get a good position after the war, but he would have been better off if he had stayed on his farm because he was missing in action soon after he joined the army. He was captured alive by German and Croatian soldiers. Marko's wife Mara, who lived in Zagreb during the war, visited him in jail. She brought food for him but was never allowed to see him. Finally the jailors wouldn't accept food anymore; therefore, Mara knew they had taken him to an unknown destination, most likely a concentration camp where his fate would end tragically.

Wars and their personal tragedies are always the same: Those who make a war don't die in it, but those who don't want it do. And families on both sides are left without fathers, sons, brothers and husbands, often without knowing their fate, hoping against hope that these loved ones may return some day.

My uncle's wife Bara waited for Stjepan a long time, but she was still young and needed to get her life in order and have children. She married Ivan Svazic from Golivrh. They had one daughter Milice after they moved to Karlovac, where they lived for the rest of their lives. The communists installed a monument *(shown above)* in Ribnik, close to Zrinski Frankopani Castle, where they imprinted the names of those killed or missing on their side in the war. Uncle Stjepan's name is first on the top.

Dragica was the eighth child born to grandparents Jagas. When she married Miho Maver before World War

II, they had two children, a son who died and a daughter Ana who is now in Kichener, Canada. *(Left: Dragica's daughter Ana and husband, Ivan Drgastin.)* Miho was due to join the army at peace time. He had a slight difficulty in hearing and should never have been called to the army, but that was close to wartime, and his problem wasn't enough excuse for him to avoid service. One evening, another soldier was guarding his troop as Miho was walking by. The soldier called, "Stop!" but Miho just kept walking because he hadn't heard. Again the soldier called, "Stop!" but Miho did not. He was shot, so fatal things occur in peace time also. And three young widows grieved in my mother's family. Neither Dragica nor Bara married after their husbands died, although they were still in their twenties when they became widows. Dragica is the only one of four sisters still alive there in Kitchener, Canada, living with her daughter Ana and husband Ivan Drgastin.

Magdalena's youngest child had married Stjepan's wife's brother, Ivan Jarnevic. That was a marriage that we Croatians call "in exchange." When a brother and sister married another brother and sister, it meant that parents on both sides could keep their properties as they were, with parents on neither side giving their daughter a portion of their property. In the Jagas family, when Stjepan was killed and his wife remarried, then my aunt Milka got her marriage portion when her parents died, and Bara got hers from her with a second marriage. Milka and Ivan had one daughter, Barica, who lived in Karlovac with her husband and two children.

I can never forget those days when I visited Golivrh. On one occasion, when I was about five years old, Mom took me and little Jure to visit the grandparents so that Jure could forget breast feeding. We stayed there about one month. Grandpa wasn't only doing business with cattle, he also was making pottery which he sold as cooking pots to ladies. Jure and I liked to play with his tools, especially with the wheel on which he turned that pottery. He forbade us to play with it unless he was supervising. Of course, we were like any other kids, not accepting his discipline, turning the wheel. He threatened to spank us both, which we deserved, but mother told me that I said, "If you are going to spank us, we will go home. Anyway, is that why we came here? So you could spank us?" Hoping to hear more funny things from me, he asked, "Do you know to get home?" I said, "I know how. Here, you will see." I took my little brother by the hand and proceeded down behind their barn, continuing downhill till grandpa had time to stop us. I told him which way our home was – first downhill, then cross the creek, then through the forest and over another creek when we would be close to our home. He had his little fun with us and a big laugh, then got us to the house and said, "You were wrong. You start to your home behind the old house." He was right, we had started the wrong way.

Grandma Magdalena had her own small business, but it paid poorly when people didn't have money. Often, people helped on the farm as payment. Grandma knew how to make clothes, but it was all hand sewing because she had no machine. She also prepared the thread for manufacturing clothes. Ladies wove their own thread from hemp fiber, then Grandma put threads together and assembled them on a loom with which ladies could weave fabric.

(In the photo at right, Ljuba [Bosiljevac] Hadusek's daughter-in-law demonstrates one part of the process used to make fabric. The family set up one room in Brdo as a family museum, although nobody lives there anymore.)

Quite an extensive process was involved before hemp fiber became fabric ready for clothes. When hemp was ready for harvesting, we picked it up, tied it into small bundles and loaded it on a wagon which oxen pulled to the Kupa River at the village of Jakovci. That part of the Kupa River looked more like a beach. There we laid the bundles down, weighted them with heavy rocks, and left them for ten days to rot inside the plants, although the fiber outside remained strong. When the plants were rotten enough, we washed the leaves away. We took home the bare white bundles, which we laid on the ground in our yards to dry out for another ten days. When the plants became brittle enough, we used our feet on a toothed breaking tool which separated the strong fiber from the already rotten plants. Next, another tool was used to smooth the fiber until it was ready for weaving. The thread was washed in acid until it became white. Grandma had a big round spinner with which she assembled threads from many balls to get one yard width of fabric. She took that to customers' houses to reassemble threads for looming. Ladies made many yards of such fabric for their families. *(When my mother came to America, she brought back some of that fabric which I still treasure as a souvenir.)*

(This loom picture was taken by Dora [Bosiljevac] Kolic's granddaughter Mary, who was vacationing in Croatia from Canada. She kindly sent pictures to Dianne [Sambol] Spehar, who allowed me to use them in this book.)

Before World War II, our ladies could buy cotton threads out of which to make fabric. These threads were much thinner and better, but what we made with our labor was free.

That was how we lived. With very little money, we bought almost nothing and were self sufficient. Our lives were interesting and peaceful. We weren't squeezed up tightly against our neighbors. That kind of life is now disappearing: We live tightly in our neighborhoods as well as on the streets. Our kids go to schools as large as factories, the shy and calm ones often bullied by arrogant children.

Grandma Magdalena was a talented lady who could do whatever she saw others doing. Mother told me that I was the only one of Grandma's grandchildren who took after her talent – to learn everything from others. Grandma was also a kind and unselfish person. We often felt sorry for her when we saw her never taking anything for herself, just giving everything to her family. She didn't even eat with children. She would say, "If anything is left over, then I will eat." Everybody knew that, so they always left her some food. My parents called her "Saint Magdalena." She had a hard life, but she was happiest at home.

A tiny lady, Grandma had green eyes and light brown hair. She was born in 1882, the same year as Grandpa. At age 70, Grandpa died of pneumonia on March 19, 1952, Saint Joseph Day. Grandma died in 1956 at age 74. Writing this memoir has renewed my memories of them, of Golivrh, and of my childhood. My grandparents were always happy and content, leaving me a legacy I cherish and will never forget.

Chapter 5: **"Our Little Croatian Corner"**

Ribnik County is a unique place in Croatia which we sometimes called "Our little Croatian corner." With infrequent tourists or business traffic, it was just a center for local people who had business with each other or a need to sell or buy goods not available on our farms. During the communist era we had one little store in Ribnik village and another close by Grice, Veselice and Jarnevice. Those stores were called Zadrugas, meaning "partnerships."

Certainly this was a word dear to the communists who pushed people to live in other "Zadrugas" or communes that they established. Their idea was for each village to form a commune, combine all farms and have all families work the land together. The communists even took land away from some local people to make the commune larger and wealthier. The idea was for the whole village to give up their land to form the Zadruga, then work the land together as one family. At harvest time, the entire crop was to go in one pile, with each person getting so many kilos to last him or her for an entire year. When the crops had been allotted, the excess was to go to the communists for use somewhere else. The plan didn't work well at all because those who were in the web of communist thought wanted to be bosses, and people who came to their communes were often poor with no experience in farm work. In Ribnik County, our people said, "No way. We would rather be poor our own way than to be poor their way." After some years, even the communists saw how poorly the plan was working, so they dismantled it and returned to allowing each owner to work the land that was his.

The plan for farmers was a failure, but the communists did succeed in taking businesses away from people. Some little stores and bars had been privately owned.

After the war, communists took everything away from the owners, In those little stores we could buy only basic necessities such as sugar, salt, and everyday items used by our people on their farms. If we needed other important things we had to go farther to Karlovac or Matlika, a little Slovenian city which was closer to us than Karlovac.

Because those of us who lived by the Kupa River had surrendered, we were protected during the war, but we still were subject to some shooting and bombing. After the war, some German tourists would pass along our highway, but not many, for the war was still on everybody's mind.

In Ribnik County, people were and still are 100% Croatian nationality and Catholic religion. That is why I say we lived in a unique place.

Lipnik church was built of solid stone during the fourteenth century. Historically, it had been wealthy, owning not only the building itself and a home for the resident priest, but acres of prime farmland as well as many acres of forest. The communists, of course, took almost all land from the church – some to keep for themselves and some for landless poor and friends of the communists. After the communists lost power, Lipnik church was recognized by the Croatian government as a national treasure. The church is still beautiful although it badly needs renovation inside and out. In the 90's, many of us who had emigrated from that parish helped renew some of the church's most deteriorated areas, such as the roof and the foundation. A large sum is still needed to get the church in decent shape. It was last painted in 1914, while the priest Belanic served. (Father Belanic, who had baptized my mother) left and was replaced by Alojz Springer.

Father Springer served in Lipnik for forty years, but never continued restoration efforts. Once in the 40's he solicited money for a new organ but the old one was never replaced. When Alojz Springer arrived, he brought with him a young lady who served as his cook. Later, his sister came with two of her children, a son and a daughter. Little was known about the family's history, but most likely his sister had lost her husband in World War I.

After the sister's arrival, she could have cooked for him and her children, but she only took care of her family while the other young lady not only continued to cook, but became the boss of all activity on the property. The priest had such authority in the parish that although we disapproved of the arrangement, we could do nothing about it. The church property contained a large farm that needed care, so the priest paid parishioners small wages to work on the farm. Before she married my father, my mother was one of those workers. She said, "When we worked on their farm, the woman who was supposed to be the cook was instead the main authority over us. She stood in front of the workers, watching us constantly to be sure that they, including me, worked fast enough to warrant what we were being paid."

Father Springer also employed a butler who drove with horses and wagon wherever the priest needed to go. He also took care of the cattle and had other responsibilities, as well. Sometimes those two argued, so Gojtan (as everyone called him) would leave, only to return every time for those forty years the priest was there.

After Father Springer's nephew, Karle Banjac, was educated and grown, he got married and opened a small clothing store on church property. His son, Ivica was my age, so he and I were in the same class in the Lipnik school. After the war, Karle and his family moved to the city, but his sister Pavlina stayed with her uncle, the priest, as long as he was there. Father Springer retired in 1955 and went to the city. Pavlina left as well and got married.

Below Lipnik forest, on the edge of the village stands Sant Ilija parish church. Almost every village has a chapel of its own, although in some instances, two small villages will have one chapel where residents may obtain an annual mass and festival. Some of these chapels are small, containing only a saint's statue placed so that it is visible through a glass door, allowing passersby to cross themselves as they pass. Other chapels are as large as a small church, where people could sit inside when mass was served.

These chapels in Ribnik County still tell us of our history -- of a time when aristocratic families lived and built their own chapels on the land with their castles. All of our villages had these local authorities who breathed down their necks day after day, forcing local people to work free for the aristocrats. Croatian history registers this as "The Slavery Era." That lasted until 1848 when Croatians, under the leadership of our hero, The Ban (Governor) Josip Jelacic, succeeded in winning the war against Hungary.

When Coatia was freed from Hungary, it was left in the Austrian Empire, and our people's lives improved – at least that is what my grandfather told us. He said, "We could sell everything we grew on our farms if we had more than we needed." Apparently they were doing well indeed, so well that as the rest of Europe was being threatened by Austrian advances, and some Europeans began planning for the first "world war."

As communism crumbled in Eastern Europe during the 1990's and Croatia struggled for independence, I became interested in Croatian history, so I looked for a library book which could tell me why World War I originated in that region. Everybody knew it started there, but I wondered, what was the real reason?

Although no one completely understands world politics, I have loved solving puzzles by digging through books to learn what is missing. Hopefully, I have been able to replace some missing pieces. Sifting through my research books, I discovered the reason to be that the Austrian Empire's strong economy was linked to rich provinces in Austria and Croatia. When Austrian Archduke Francis Ferdinand and his wife Sophie were killed in Sarajevo, Bosnia, by Serbian nationalists, this provided a good enough reason for Austrians to declare war on Serbia. Perhaps they were naïve to suspect Serbs were playing the role alone. Other countries were waiting for just such a line from Austria, whose economy was threatening their own.

The post-World-War-I map was redrawn again, as it had been so many times previously. Croatia and Bosnia were switched to the Balkans, along with Slovenia which had been under Italian control until 1918, when Yugoslavia was created. Those nations who were threatened by the rich Austrian Empire needed to be careful to avoid creating such power any more. Croatia, which was rich with Slavonia's top quality agricultural land and the Dalmatian Ocean's large tourism attraction, were pushed to the poor Balkans, where their resources were distributed among less fortunate nations.

In 1918, world powers were deciding to push Croatia into Yugoslavia, which would have made six states whose people didn't have the same language or even the same alphabet. President Woodrow Wilson of the United States was the only one who wasn't in favor of this decision. He pointed out that Croatia would be shifted from one depression to another. Russia, France and England wouldn't allow Croatia to exist as a free country, so Croatia became subject to yet another power, Yugoslavia, whose leader was King Alexander of Serbia. Small nations work constantly to fend off foreign occupation, so Croatian peasant party leader Stjepan Radic and some of his associates were unhappy about uniting Croatia with the Serbian kingdom. King Alexander invited Radic to Belgrade to negotiate. When Radic and his advisers arrived, he was shot in parliament on June 20th and died August 8, 1928. Yet again, the Croatian people had lost a great leader for the same cause. They had lost Croatia as their real country in 1102 when Hungary took away their independence, and in 1928, they failed to get it back again.

As they had under other foreign occupiers, Croatians felt deep pain in every corner of their land. No help from the federal government ever came to Ribnik County, though the farmers were taxed heavily on the few acres they owned. If the summer weather was good, people could at least grow enough food to sustain their families, but if the crops were poor, they still had to pay the same taxes as in good, rainy summers. None of the foreign governments ever allotted money to local counties, money which could have been used to install electricity, piped water and telephones – basics which would have relieved some of the farmers' hardships. We never even thought of having paved roads, but if they had been available we would have thought we were in heaven. Local governments didn't even repair the roads that existed; they just ordered each family to repair ten or twenty meters of the county road themselves.

If such basic things had been available, we might have been able to have small shops where people could make a little money. That might have helped us stay in the place where we were born. Instead, we scattered over different continents or just moved to Croatian cities in which we were able to survive on small wages.

Thankfully, today Croatia is an independent country. Its politicians do more for their citizens than foreigners ever did. It would be easier, however, to provide basic services if the county were still full of people. Although there are only a few families left in Ribnik County, the local government has installed those things they needed. Croatia has done more for the people in ten years than previous governments did in centuries.

In 1957 electricity was installed In Ribnik County, paid for the people themselves during the communist era. Since Croatia gained independence, they have water from pipes, telephones and paved county roads. If small countries become independent after many years of depression, it takes a long time to get out of the miserable conditions in which their occupiers left them. Since so few residents remain, it is difficult for the local government to raise enough tax money to help, but they are managing to do better.

Some villages, however, have completely disappeared from the map, such as Golivrh, the village in which my mother was born, and only two people now live on Brdo. It is the same story in many villages, not only in Ribnik County, but all over Croatia.

When I was growing up, we were acquainted with families throughout Ribnik County, and all of our lives were centered on our churches and chapels. For us, of course, that center was Saint Ilija Church in Lipnik. The house closest to Saint Ilija Church belonged to Stjean Car, whose brothers and sisters immigrated here in Kansas City. Later, as my husband and I came, Stjepan's two sons settled here also.

Stjepan was the main layman in our church in Croatia when I lived there and he remained there long after I had left. Besides serving the priest during mass, he pulled the rope in order to ring the steeple bell at noon so we knew when to leave the fields for lunch and again in the evening so we could stop work and head home. The sound of the bell was more sentimental than practical, but it was enjoyable to hear. Sometimes we couldn't hear that bell from Lipnik church because we were far away and the wind was blowing from the south toward the church, but we had our Saint Ana chapel in which another person rang that bell. Other family names in Lipnik included Samovojska, Jacmenovic and Bozic.

The next village in the county was named Skratsko Selo. People who lived there had the names Skratski, Kralj, Frankovic and Staresinic. A little farther in was the little village of Kamenak. People there were named Lister, Dolinar and Modrcin. Then farther toward Ribnik were two small villages close together named Drenovice and Ramnice. The family surnames there were Gorup, Muljak and Ropar. The villages named here are on low land by our highway, about in the middle of County Ribnik.

Our parish church provided the perfect place for parishioners to socialize after services. Those of us from our little villages might never have known each other if we hadn't met there. Two giant linden trees towered next to the church, and it was there we stopped to chat with relatives and friends for some time before heading home. Everyone enjoyed standing under those trees, breathing the scents from Lipnik forest which stretched from the church property as far as the Kupa River across a high hill. We children learned the names of those from other villages by asking our parents who they were. Now, if anybody in Kansas City asks me where in Ribnik County their relative with a certain name lived, I can tell which village from those conversations I heard after church when I was young.

During the first half of the 20th century, we ladies dressed up for church in special clothes which were unique to our parish. Our mothers had to buy special materials for these, which imposed a financial hardship, but mother didn't seem to mind. I was a lucky girl, thankful to have relatives in America, Uncle Marko and Aunt Mary Bosiljevac, who were sensitive to such needs and sent this fabric. Several years after World War II, when we young people from the countryside mixed with those from cities, we began adopting clothing styles like theirs. Our mothers pushed us to stay with tradition, at least in church, but they had little success. We were determined to continue wearing city styles.

Every year our church sponsored a festival on Saint Izidor Day because one altar, though not the main one, is of that saint. That day is still very popular. Those who live in Croatian cities come every year to enjoy the traditional celebration as did their parents and grandparents. (Those of us who now live on other continents often plan our trips back there to coincide with such traditions.) The festival brought joy to those of every age, especially the children, who asked parents to buy them sweet pastries and drinks. Tables were set up under those two linden trees for the festivities. Lunch featured roasted pigs and lambs, and afterwards, many people danced till late at night. No one had much money, but they saved for such rare activities so they could have a good time and visit with friends, old and new.

Such church gatherings did provide some relief for the families in Ribnik County. Although most were small farmers, there were also some little shops in which usually one person worked for himself. Blacksmiths, wagon makers, barrel makers and others provided some of the things which were vital to the farmers.

Before the war, Rudof and Katarina Zrinski, with their little daughter Branka, had a store by our highway, not far from Grice in a place named Graban. During the war, Rudof and two other men, Miko Hadusek and Miko Dolinar were gunned down on our highway by men in the opposing army. Miko Hadusek had a brother Juro here in Kansas City, and Miko Dolinar had two sisters here, Mary Novosel and Kathy Modrcin. All three of them had family in Grice and Lipnik, but those who killed them had no feeling for their wives or small children.

Rudof and his wife had no land; they were just living in the little store which Katarina ran after her husband was killed. Although I was still a small child during the war, I remember visiting that store, filled with the warm smell of coffee, and I remember Katarina's graciousness when she served us. After the war, communists took the store from her. They didn't even allow Katarina to continue working in it to make a scant living for herself and Branka. Katarina wasn't a person with a friendly face, nor was her daughter, but when people needed them they were courteous and helpful, which surprised everyone. Because they lived right by the highway, a mail car had a stop for pickup and delivery right by their place. During the winter months, it was too cold to wait outside; therefore we would just come to wait for the postman in the little kitchen in which they lived. They never turned us down, and never complained that we were in their way, which, of course, we were.

Being shy, I hardly ever spoke to Branka, who was a few years older, but to my surprise, on one occasion she showed a kindness toward me. When I was fourteen, the government ordered us teenage girls to take first aid classes at our local school. Our teacher was a friend of Branka's then. Our teacher was preparing us girls and boys to perform in a show at an upcoming dance in newly built hall which sat at the intersection of Netrtic County. Young people were expected at the dance from as far away as Karlovac. We were looking forward to being there, too, but we were very nervous about performing. The show was really simple, with a lead girl and a boy singing as they talked to each other. The boy was easy to choose; Mike Zeleznjak was known for his good voice. But, deciding on the girl wasn't so simple because none of us had a good voice. Branka was helping the teacher select one of us. After we tried out for the part, I was greatly surprised when Branka said, "Ana is the one who is the best." I certainly didn't have a good voice for singing, but Branka saw something in me that she thought could carry it off. We will never know, since the show was canceled because of a lack of needed equipment. In one way I was glad, because my cold feet matched my soft voice, but still it was a disappointment.

Some years later, when we grew to be young women, Branka made a beautiful, deep rose-colored decorative pillow for my bridal bedroom. After fifty years, I still have that thoughtful gift which is one piece of my marriage memories. My mother brought it to America when she and my father came in 1967.

(Above: The decorative pillow is one treasured souvenir from my marriage to Ivan.)

Nobody in Ribnik County owned a car right after the war. No local traffic ran on our highway, although once in a while a car would appear, not owned by local people but by someone from a city who was just passing through. In later years a bus would stop at Grice on selected days so people could get to Karlovac without walking the nineteen kilometers. Before the war I was still too little to walk that far, but afterwards I walked sometimes.

I remember my first walk to Karlovac when my cousin Ana Svazic sent this message from Zagreb to my mother: *"Dear Aunt Mara, as we couldn't communicate during this vicious war with us here in Zagreb not knowing if you are fine or not and you not knowing if we are fine or not, we now know that you are alive and Uncle Janko, even if he is still in the army, is alive, also. Therefore I wish to see at least you and your children. Would you, dear aunt, bring the children to Karlovac to meet me at our cousin Ljubica's, where I could come easier than to your house in Grice?"* Aunt Ljubica had two houses, one in Karlovac which she used as a rental and another in a suburb called Kalvarija, where she and the rest of her family lived. My mother took Drago, age 12 and me, age 10. Jure, who was only 7 couldn't go that far but, as it turned out, we couldn't either! We did manage to walk to Karlovac and had our family reunion, but returning home, mother was in trouble even before we left the city. She didn't know what to do with us because our shoes were already giving us blisters. She looked for somebody from our area, and luckily she found a friend with a horse and wagon who did give us a ride. My first trip to Karlovac was certainly painful enough for me to remember well, even all of these years later.

In addition to some sections of land in our chestnut forest, the Bosiljevac family also had one parcel of beach trees in the Lipnik forest. That piece of land was on top of a hill some distance from our home. When we decided to go there to cut wood to warm our home, we prepared ourselves and our oxen for nearly an entire day. As I got older, I helped the men bring that wood home. Sometimes my father and Drago went ahead to cut trees down, and I followed them with our oxen and wagon. These were my special days as the team and I wound our way up there from Brdo. As I was very familiar with the area, I knew there was nothing to fear in the forest, not even a wolf, although one had come close enough to startle me some years before.

I enjoyed the complete silence around me as I strolled through the forest with the oxen and wagon. Occasionally a rabbit would jump here and there in our path, and birds of different colors would swoop above us. In the silence of the forest I had no distractions, and I could pursue my own thoughts as nature's beauty sank deep into my body and my brain. The birds and the wind flapping the forest leaves gave me the complete peace I always adored.

(Oxen still helped my famiy with chores in the 1950's.)

Our oxen were very tame and already knew the way, so they just followed for about an hour, until we reached the true Lipnik forest. Here, the road seemed more like a city street, level and smooth. That was my favorite part of the forest. Beach trees towered high in the sky. Although their large lower trunks were leafless, a canopy of leaves at the tops covered the sky, allowing the sun to peer mysteriously through the greenery. Sometimes I was able to see a mother vulture sitting on her nest, guarding her babies. It was interesting to see these birds, nesting or flying through the sky on their large wings, although our mothers had a different opinion because vultures sometimes took our baby chickens.

We had a hard time protecting the eggs until they hatched and the young ones grew up.

Reaching the top of the forest area, I could hear the echoing sounds of my family's voices and their axes. I would stop to listen for awhile, to hear if others were in the area. My father and brother now had the task of loading the wood, which gave me time of my own to stroll through the forest. On a sunny spring day, I would look up to see leaves fluttering in the mild south breeze. Nature, I wondered, how could it be so beautiful and so gentle some of the time and so rough other times and in other places? We are part of the nature around us, and I believe God gave us the obligation to take care of things we see, use, breathe and drink so that future generations will have a clean environment forever.

Most of our forest property was in a deep, heavily wooded area on relatively level surface, but one section was in a deep valley where it was painful to get wood. When we cut wood in that part, we discovered pieces of ore in the ground. I was glad that nobody suggested mining that hill, which would have ruined the beauty of the area. There are many abusers of nature in this beautiful world, but there is no true wealth other than the loveliness of what God has provided for us. Our only responsibility is to preserve and take care of it.

When my two men had loaded the cut wood on the wagon, it was time to head home. We would then pass by an area named Brezovkal, which means birch pond. From here we could see how the Kupa River wound below, far away around three sides of Ribnik County and then flowed on to Karlovac. This would be an ideal location for a tourist hotel, and visitors probably would flock there if only the county could afford to build roads into the area. Most of this enchanting place belonged to the people of St. Katerina. *(Many people from that parish immigrated to Kansas City, from villages named*

Pekici, Pavecic, Kunic, Juratovic, Bogovci and Mrzljaki. Surnames in those villages included Pekic, Pavic, Pavecic, Pavlic, Pavlovic, Kovacid, Kucenic, Kovac, Horvat, Sestric, Novogradac, Janakovic, Juratovic, Kralj, Trzok, Fabina, Suljak, Demor, and Levojevic.)

Looking toward Bosnia from there, we would ask the older people the name of the mountain in the distance. They told us, "That is the mountain piled up from the dirt the Turks brought on their moccasins." This wry little joke referred to the place where the Turks plundered during their occupation of Bosnia.

On a clear day, we could see even beyond Karlovac from this spot, although we couldn't see the city itself because it is cut off from view by a hill on our side. Karlovac is on very low land, where four rivers flow together.

Ribnik County still bears visible traces of the area's history. Our parents and grandparents had told us about the aristocratic authorities that controlled the lives of every family. We of a younger generation could still see remnants of their properties in Grice, although only the old St. Ana's Chaple still stands in fair condition, but the present owner of that property has forbidden the people and the priest to use it, but in the village of Ribnik their castle still stands.

After the lords were gone, the Croatian authorities sold such properties to local people. Those who had come home from America with some money bought most of that property. A man named Drago Kralj bought many of these landmarks. Because he remained in America with his family, he asked my grandfather Tomo to take care of the property, selling hay from the large yard and repairing buildings. When the chaple needed a new roof, Grandpa borrowed money from the bank and covered the chaple with some special tin which is still on that roof. When Drago Kralj decided to stay in America permanently, he asked Grandpa to buy the property from him. Grandpa decided to do it, but Grandma's neighbors and friends began calling her "Madam" because she would live in the former lord's home, and they were probably jealous. She didn't want to seem different from her friends, so Grandpa let that beautiful property's ownership pass by them. In the 70's, my brother Jure had the opportunity to buy it, but he was dissuaded by our father, who lived in Kansas City. Jure was living in Ljubljana, Slovenia, at the time, and father convinced Jure that the property needed someone who could live there and take care of it, not one who lived a busy life in another area. Finally a local family named Zeleznjak bought it and forbade people of the area to use it even once a year on the Sunday following July 26th, known as St. Ana's Day.

Ribnik County remains closely related to Kansas City, because almost every surname of Ribnik County is represented here. We can see this clearly on the stones in our cemetery at 38th Street and State Avenue. Croatia is a small country, but many, many acres of its land lie there unused because so much of the population left those small farms -- some for cities in Croatia and some scattered to other countries, even other continents -- all seeking lives with more opportunity than they had in their homeland.

(Note also the register on page 267 of Lipnik County surnames.)

Those of us who have emigrated from Croatia generally have easier lives now, but the memories and the beauty of our native land still call to our hearts and souls.

Chapter 6: **World War II Reaches Us**

Even when Europe was becoming a hot spot, war was unknown in our area. Only five years old in 1940, I was hardly aware of anything outside of our quiet farm lives, but I remember vividly the St. Ana's Festival that year. Usually this was a happy time, but that year I became aware that things were turning out just the opposite.

For that festival, people came from far away for mass. Those who had relatives in the area were invited to stay for lunch. My father was in some kind of army, but for the celebration, mother took us children for an afternoon with her sisters and brother Stjepan. Grandma Jagas came every year on July 26th to attend confession and mass with the priest. Then she came to our house, bringing cake for my name day.

On the following Sunday, the younger generation gathered for other festivities. A dance floor had been built under that apple tree where Drago Bosiljevac and I had gotten in trouble with Drago Zaleznjak. Everyone with children had brought their little ones without any worries. As the dancing began, my mother sat chatting with her relatives and friends, sipping cool drinks while we children ran through the yard playing. Suddenly, everybody began hurrying to one place in the distance. Curious, we children followed, digging between people's legs to see what was happening. I could not understand, but I remember seeing a grown man lying on the ground with his brown shoes pointing up. He was dead. Adults were crying and yelling, "A man has been killed!"

Many people in our area were good natured, hard working, but there were also others who were arrogant and who drank too much. The center of the argument was a young lady whose husband had emigrated to

Argentina *(and who had "forgotten" he had a wife at home)*. Single men had been competing for favors from her that they couldn't get from the single girls. Two of the men who had been drinking started shouting. Unfortunately, both had guns and began to shoot, then ran away. But Ivan Ratkaj, an innocent bystander, was killed. He was from the village Mrtinskl Vrh, located on the highest point in our county. Two of Ivan's sisters, Ljuba Jarmek and Ana Fabac, lived in Grice. For years after this event, we all would see and hear their grief over the senseless death of their innocent young brother.

In 1943, when I was only eight years old, World War II was raging all over Europe, but there was no military activity in Ribnik County. My father said that the Italian army was in Karlovac and the state of Slovenia across the Kupa River, but it meant little to me until I watched my mother cry as her brother Stjepan Jagas marched down our highway with other volunteers to join the partizan forces. They had been persuaded that the war would be over soon, and then they would have the opportunity for government jobs that would free them from hard farm labor. That was the first group of volunteers in our county, and the last volunteers for either side in the conflict.

People in Croatia were confused during World War II. We didn't like the partizans because they were communists, but the partizans did fight with the western countries against the Germans. Our people knew if the west won the war we would have to stay as part of Yugoslavia, which would be communist. On the other hand, those who fought on the German side thought they would have a free Croatia, which many of us wished for. Those who fought on the partisan side were the winners with a leader Tito, who was also a communist, so the Croatian people were left in the communist bloc, isolated from the west, including America. The communists oppressed us like never before, so we asked ourselves were we really the winners? We felt we could not be winners no matter with which side we had fought. That is why our people hid from both sides, just as my father did until the partizans took him from his niece's house.

Still, partizans hunted young men to get them to join their side. To avoid this, some of our men hid in our forest, digging bunkers under the ground in which they could hide, at least temporarily . . . until they were discovered. In our neighborhood, we saw how Mara Bosiljevac hid her son Mirko inside their barn. She even asked my mother to let her son sleep in our spare house through the night. My mother helped her neighbor as much as she could, but she feared the partizans would find out because they had already come to ask her where her husband was. Four young men, including Mara's son, dug a bunker in the forest where they hid. Nobody knew where it was, not even their families, but one evening when Janko Klemencic was visiting his home, somebody was watching. Janko was arrested and forced to take the partisans to where his friends were hiding. They all were arrested and taken away.

Downstream on the Kupa River was the next county to ours, named Ozalj. Quartered there was the army which collaborated with the Germans. Men from Ribnik County who lived close to Ozalj had also joined this group. They didn't really understand any political side, but they had to join one or the other, and this one was closer to their homes. To these men, whatever seemed to fit more by allowing them, they hoped, to help feed their families and warm their homes in the winter was the better choice. Since they had no access to newspapers, radio or television, informed decisions were unavailable to them. They didn't want to be on either side, but many of them died on both sides before the war was over.

During the fall of 1943, the war came to Ribnik County. I don't remember everything in order, but one incident is still very clear in my mind. My father had gotten on top of our walnut tree to shake walnuts down to mother, Drago and me. We were on our land down by St. Ana's Chapel, and Grandfather and little Jure were with our cattle close to the road. As father slid down from the tree to help us on the ground, we spotted a whole long line of partizans and their mules coming down from Upper Grice. As the partizans came closer, father recognized one man with whom he had previously served in the regular army. Stepping closer, father and the soldier shook hands as father told mother how he knew this man.

We watched for a while as the men marched down the road with their equipment-laden mules. As they passed by our property where neighbors' children were with their cattle, an airplane suddenly emerged very low on the opposite side over the forest hill. Father said, "I am afraid something bad is going to happen."

And it did -- so fast that nobody had much time to get away from that site. The plane passed over our heads only to turn around. Father warned, "He is going to bomb the area because of those soldiers!" People were working, and children were watching cattle all over the meadow, but those in the air didn't care who could die. Father ordered mother and us children to walk toward our home, then he ran down toward Grandfather and little Jure to get them away from the road where soldiers were marching. Grandpa, who was old and never afraid of anything, said, "Why run away? This is nothing." But as father pulled him and Jure away, two bombs fell on the spot where they had been standing. Another two bombs fell on St. Ana's property, where neighborhood children were. The older children ran, but four-year-old Mirko Hadusek got only as far as a bush about 100 feet away from where the bombs dug a large hole in the ground. Two bombs fell on our school property on the other side of the highway; two more fell on Josip Novosel's barn, but did not explode. Amazingly, neither we nor those soldiers were hurt, but it scared all of us badly. As we walked toward home, I saw bombs flying two by two all over our area. That scene is still in front of my eyes when I remember it.

Later in the fall, my father disappeared. I don't remember his saying goodbye to us, though he probably did to mother. We children were not told because he had gone secretly to his niece in a suburb of Karlovac. Partizans were hunting men from the villages, but father, like other farmers, didn't want to fight for either side. In Karlovac, where the Germans were, father got help from his niece and her friend's doctor, who gave father an exemption so he would not have to serve in any army. Mother told us where father was; she also told partizans that he wasn't in the opposing army, although they didn't believe her.

Another time in 1943, Germans and Croatians came from Karlovac looking for partizans. Often they had come as far as Grice and had stayed for three or four days. This was the only time when they came to Upper Grice, where partizans sometimes had settled in somebody's house. When we saw their vehicles, which looked like tanks only lighter and more open, we were afraid they would hurt some of us. We had never expected for them to come to Brdo, which was very hilly and the road was narrow and rocky, but that didn't stop them. They just drove their vehicles through our hills and fields. As we children saw them coming, we ran to our homes to be with our families.

My grandma was the only adult at home when two young German soldiers arrived at our home, well dressed in their uniforms. When grandma stepped out on the porch to meet them, I went out with her to see these soldiers from another country for the first time. I stayed close to her apron as they stepped on our porch with pistols in their hands. In answer to their question, "Partizans? Partizans?" -- the only word they knew in our language -- Grandma replied, "No partizans." They pushed past her and opened the door on a little room where she kept bread and eggs in a chest. They did take a few eggs, but then they left. Neighbors told us how those soldiers later sat on some logs in Petar Hrastovcak's courtyard, tossing our eggs from one man to another without breaking them. The Germans didn't stay long, just going through Upper Grice that first and last time. In my memory I can still see them clearly and remember every move they made.

We had no communication with father, and couldn't let him know when his mother became gravely ill. Although she was twelve years younger than her husband, Grandma had diabetes. Because of the war, we couldn't take her to Karlovac, with its hospital and doctors. During this time, when our people became seriously ill, they just died, because medical help was not available. My mother was the only one who could help her in and out of bed, since Grandpa was eighty years old and we children were all too young. Others in our village had family members to help in such cases, but mother did not, so for eleven weeks mother handled all the family responsibilities and graciously tended her mother-in-law. Before she became ill, Grandma had fell she was the authority in our house and hadn't respected my mother. She often had given mother a hard time. She had told mother that she wouldn't need her in her own old age because she had nieces who would take care of her if needed. And as long as Grandma was well, the nieces had visited her, but now that she needed them, they hardly came, having their own family responsibilities. So now, twelve years after my parents married, Grandma said, "My dear daughter, what would I do if I didn't have you these hard days?" She had never before called my mother "daughter."

Grandfather was a different type of person. He was kind and honest. Mother had only kind words to say for him. He also had a difficult time with Grandma, but at least she was good to us children. She loved us and was always kind to us, often protecting us from older kids. I don't understand why she couldn't accept my mother; perhaps she didn't know any better. My mother believed that God will reward us for "patient salvation." Mother had done everything possible for Grandma during her last illness, making her last days comfortable.

Grandmother Bosiljevac died during Holy Week in the spring of 1944. She had hated the partizans when she was alive because she had to cook free meals for them even though she had difficulties feeding her own family. Ironically, after she died, a partizan soldier was killed in our area and was buried next to Grandma. She wouldn't have liked it if she knew, but when the war was over, the partizan's family claimed his body and buried him in their cemetery in the village of Prilisce. The man's name was Nikola Oreskovic.

Eventually, father was able to send us a few things such as salt, sugar and petroleum for our lamps. Most of our people didn't have even those things. During the war we had only those foods which we produced on our land and the clothes we had manufactured ourselves. People today might think it would be impossible to live under those conditions, but I know it is possible because we lived in them.

We children could do little to help with the house or farm, but Drago and I continued going to school until our teacher was called to join the army and our local school was closed for a year. Our mother, to whom education was always important, sent us to Lipnik school, the same one she and father had attended when they were children. It was more than a one-hour walk each way, but at least we continued learning.

Sometimes German and Croatian soldiers came from Karlovac to our place looking for partizans; other times they passed by Grice, and sometimes they would shoot up toward our houses from the highway. Occasionally they stayed three or four days in Car Valley at the family home of Stanko Kralj. That house was on a higher point, from which they could see all over Upper Grice. Even though I was only eight, I remember one of those occasions clearly, and I'm certain everybody in Brdo remembered as well.

Grandfather and I were in our yard behind the house. The yard sloped down to a little valley bordering the property of Stjepan Bosiljevac. Grandpa was cutting the grass with a scythe *(I don't know how he did that at age 80)* while I spread it in order to promote drying. Suddenly from the German and Croatian army station in Grice, one Croatian soldier walked on the path very close to us, with his gun on his shoulder. He probably was on his way to Brdo, but spotting grandfather, he stopped and asked him to come up to him. Grandpa Tomo said, "You are younger than I am. You come down if you need to talk to me." At that, the soldier recognized Grandpa as a growly old man who wasn't afraid to die, so the soldier turned away and proceeded to our neighborhood. A short time later he returned with our neighbor, Stjepan Bosiljevac. We wondered where the soldier was taking him. Later, we found out the real story, which shook up our community. To Stjepan, identifying a dead body didn't seem like the worst thing in his life, but it turned out to be when he saw that it was his nephew, Mato Bosiljevac, who had a wife and four children under eleven years of age. Unable to grow enough food for his family, Mato had volunteered to be a messenger for the partizans. We knew he did that so he could stay home to work on his farm. Sometimes we had seen Mato running from his home to the forest, hiding from the opposite army, but this time he had run too late. Soldiers killed him on the edge of Mato Hadusek's field, just four feet from one of my family's fields. The soldiers buried him on the spot where he was killed, but after they left his family dug him up and buried him in the cemetery.

In this war as in all of them, tragedies occurred on both sides. Three innocent people died when Stanko Kralj and his daughter-in-law were picked up from their home along with their neighbor, Bara Fabac. They were taken to Karlovac because the ladies' husbands and Stanko's son were in the partizans. On the other side, when Croatian soldiers and their families tried to escape from Tito's army, many of them were killed.

Every war leaves one generation of children with a terrible sense of loss and sadness. Some might think that children will forget, but those shocking things I witnessed in that war will stay in my head and heart forever.

Although our workforce was not adequate, at least we had plenty of rain for our crops during the war years. When partizans were stationed in nearby villages, our mothers, busy with work on the farms, sent us children to take food to the partizans, as they had ordered. Often it was the only food they had. Sometimes we had to take it two or three miles from our homes to Netretice County, an area that was sometimes not safe because of shooting. Once we took food where the partizans were saddled up at one family's home in the village of Modospotok. As the soldiers were eating under an apple tree, an airplane suddenly emerged over the mountain, headed toward us. Luckily, plenty of fruit trees covered that area and the soldiers tried to protect us children as well as themselves. Each one grabbed a child in his arms and ran under the roof of the house for cover. We were all frightened, but for us children it was again a threat like the one in which Grice had been bombed.

Another time, I believe the last time we took food to the soldiers, we were ordered by the partizans to take our food to the village of Pekici, on another side of the forest. It was farther away than we had gone before, but mother assumed that we would be with many other people, a number of them much older than I, so she thought it would be safe.

When we arrived there, we experienced lots of confusion. The war was coming to an end, and the partizans had ordered food from many villages for a meal before they left the area for the last time and went on across the Kupa River to Slovenia. We were farther from home there, and it was getting close to dark, but we had to stay as soldiers kept coming for a last meal, and we were told to wait to take our empty dishes home. When I located my dish, however, someone else's food was in it. Being young, I didn't know what to do, but my friends told me to go home with the rest of the crowd and dump the food in some bushes when we were far enough away. I vaguely remember that my friend Drago Bosiljevac was walking with me. It seemed like a good plan, but two young soldiers saw us and told us to take the dish back so the food could be eaten. I tried to explain, but in vain. I was, they said, to return and wait until that food was eaten.

Drago and I were both young children, and the idea of our having to wait and go back alone through that forest after dark was terrifying. The fear became so terrible for me, as a nine-year-old, that for years after I dreamed of being lost in that forest until I would wake up, still in painful fright.

But, as we followed those soldiers, we met two girls from Lower Grice, Mara Novosel and Ana Vidervolj, who would later marry brothers – Mara would marry Ivan Zeleznjak and Ana Stjepan. They asked me why I was going back with those soldiers, and I explained. They said, "Look. Those soldiers aren't paying attention to whether you follow them or not. Turn back with us and dump that food. The soldiers will never notice as they talk and laugh together." So I did. What a relief for Drago and me when we walked back home with those teenage girls who were courageous enough to rescue two little children.

Fortunately, in my whole life, when I am in real difficulty, God is there to rescue me, as he did then. When my life was hard, God helped me through it. When my life was unpleasant, God saw that I came out fine.

During World War II, most of the events that affected our village occurred in 1944. One that will stay with me forever happened as we children and our mother were working on one of our fields named Strmac, which means "slope." That was the field in which Mato Bosiljevac had been killed just a few months earlier. Usually, after we picked up the corn, we prepared the land for the wheat during the fall. The airplane which flew over our heads that day was not an unusual sight, but when we spotted smoke shooting out of the plane, then it definitely became unusual. Almost every day we had seen groups of planes carrying bombs, flying over us toward Germany, but they flew very high in the air. We watched closely after that heavy smoke appeared, watching it fly toward Netretic County, then back toward us. Over our heads, parachutes opened, one after another, until seven crewmen got down, scattering all over Grice and Jarnevice. The airplane landed in Netretic County, about two miles from our village. We had no idea who the survivors were, but our people searched everywhere for them. My family and I went home to eat lunch and rest before we returned for our afternoon work. When we did return, we saw one man from Upper Grice walking by with three of the soldiers who had fallen from that airplane. They didn't talk at all, so we knew they must be from another country, most likely Italy, which was closest. As we didn't have a telephone, our curiosity had to wait a long time for the answers.

Eventually we found out that one of the parachutes had fallen in the forest near Jarnevic, but people couldn't find a soldier anywhere. Thinking about neighbors who had immigrated to Kansas City, they called Stjepan Jarnevic to see if the soldier hiding under leaves and green branches was an American. Stjepan called out in English, telling the man not to be afraid of their people, and the man came out from under the branches.

Now that people knew who the men were, they took all seven to a lady named Mary Secen. She lived with her little son Paul in the village of Sopci Vrh. All of the airmen were found safe and met each other in Mary's house. They were surprised when Mary was able to communicate so well with them in English. Mary's parents, whose surname was Kralj, immigrated to Kansas City when Mary was a small child, but they left her with relatives in Croatia so they could work freely in America, thinking to bring her later. After they arrived in Kansas City, their family grew as every year they had another child, so it took them a long time to send for Mary. When she was a teenager, her parents finally brought her to America, but according to her, she didn't want to come even then. Her uncle and aunt were so good to her, she told me, that she thought of them as her mother and father.

When she arrived in this country, she was grown up and nice looking, so boys were after her for marriage. Joe Secen was the first to court her, but his brother Paul was more aggressive, so he won Mary's affection over from Joe. When Mary and Paul were married, they had one son, Paul, and lived in Kansas City for a few years, but Mary found the climate difficult for her asthma.

They returned to Sopci Vrh where they purchased property. In 1939 Paul heard that war was coming close to their country, so he left Croatia and returned to Kansas City to avoid it. He didn't avoid it, however -- he just came to it. Paul was drafted and served in

Casablanca, Africa, during the war. Mary and their son remained in Croatia during the entire war, but Mary still remembered the English she had learned during her years in America. She enjoyed conversations with the American soldiers and waited anxiously to find out what part of America they were from. She told them how she, with her husband and son had come from Kansas City, leaving their large group of relatives there. One of the soldiers said he was from Kansas City, Missouri! When he asked for her family's name, she said their surname was Kraile *(They had changed it from Kralj)* and that was also her maiden name. The soldier looked surprised and said, "I know a John Kraile in Kansas City. Is he someone you would know?" and she smiled, replying, "Well, yes. He is my brother." Could anyone have predicted such a pleasant surprise?

Mary assured the men that they were safe with her people who would take them to Slovenia, just across the Kupa River. They would then be handed to authorities who would take them to Italy, the place they had been stationed.

After that plane crashed, about two miles from Grice, our people went over there to see the smashed airplane, taking some parts as souvenirs and some for the aluminum. One man from Golivrh made cooking pots to sell out of those parts. Grandma Jagas bought two pots from him, happily demonstrating to us how strong they were. She would throw them on the floor, saying, "Look! They won't break." As long as she lived she continued cooking in those pots made from the American plane.

We were pleased to save those American soldiers, including the special man who had connected with Croatians from Ribnik County in Kansas City. I was nine years old then. It would have been interesting if I could have predicted my future. Had a fortune teller told me that I would be in Kansas City after the war, I would have jumped at the opportunity to know if that American soldier survived.

Mary Secen and her twelve-year-old son Paul returned to Kansas City right after the war. Mary's husband Paul had survived, and the family was reunited in 1946. I was too young to have known Mary in Croatia, but I heard the story of her connection with one of the Americans. After my husband and I immigrated, we rented an apartment from the Secens. Our apartment was on the second floor, and Mary and Paul lived on the first. That really was where I learned the details about that event during the war. My first question to Mary concerned that airman. Did they find out if he survived and if he did, had anybody in her family seen him? With a pleasant smile, Mary said, "My family sees him all the time, and we often have conversation about that event."

While we lived in that apartment, I had the opportunity to meet some of Mary's sisters, especially Rosy, who had three children, two boys and a girl. The girl's name became special in Kansas City: Carole Marinovich was not only the first mayor of Croatian descent, but also the first female mayor in Kansas City, Kansas history. Mayor Marinovich is praised for bringing the Kansas City Speedway to the area, and for encouraging many other businesses to follow in Village West. A nice lady, Mary Secen lived long enough to watch the development of these accomplishments.

Usually, Christmas was an enjoyable time for us Croatians, but one Christmas Eve during the war was certainly not enjoyable, for bullets flew all over our area. Partizans had recruited our men to dig a trench across the highway to stop the opposing army from using it. When they got to that point the two sides started shooting at each other. Father wasn't home then, but mother and the three of us children quickly ran to the basement. There was no inside door between the rooms inside and the basement, to we had to go outside to get there. Grandfather refused to join us. When the shooting began, he just said, "I don't care if I die or not." As I ran outside, I heard the sound of a shell flying close to my head. That scared me so much that the next day during Christmas dinner, I ran to the basement again and stayed there, so the family brought my dinner to me.

After the war, Yugoslav communists brought some German prisoners to Grice to rebuild a bridge which had been destroyed during the fighting. I remember they brought Germans to eat some fruit from our yard. By that time, the Germans could speak a little of our language. Some of them even married Croatian girls in Karlovac and remained there to live. One German told some young men from Grice that a Croatian lady had saved his life in Karlovac, so he repaid her by marrying her. When she had a baby, he shared the good news with his coworkers, saying, "My wife had a small man." All of us sound funny when we speak another language.

As during all of those winters in the 1940's, in 1944 winter snow was in full power, covering the ground as we stayed inside most of the time. Christmas was sad in those uncertain days. Grandfather grew weaker and weaker, we children were lonely, and mother worried constantly about father, of whom we knew nothing.

However, right after the New Year in 1945, somebody brought mother a message from father. He was on his way to the war. The message said for mother to come across the forest to the village of Kunice, where father and other men on their way to war would pass by. Mother took little son Drago and went through heavy snow, not knowing where father was or what she would find. When they arrived by St. Katarina church it was almost dark, but they just kept walking. They arrived a little late at their destination, only to hear that the army had already left for an unknown destination. It was bitter news for mother, of course, and she may have thought God wasn't helping her. But things don't always happen as we think they will . . .

With their officers walking in front of them, the column marched raggedly through the darkening landscape. Realizing this, father had jumped behind a bush heavy with snow and stayed there until everybody else cleared out of the area. Then he turned toward home. Walking on the road close to darkness, he spotted a lady and a little boy walking toward him. Afraid to be recognized, father pulled his coat over his face, so mother didn't know him. He, however, had recognized mother and Drago and whispered, "This is me, Janko." Then he told them to walk a little farther before turning back to catch up with him. God had indeed answered mother's prayer, not in her way, but in His.

When mother and Drago arrived home with father, Jure and I, along with grandfather Tomo, were completely surprised and happy, especially grandfather who had thought he probably would die before father came home. Father had said a few words with us and moved to get warm by the clay built stove when a knock came at the door. It was our neighbor, Mara Bosiljevac, and mother let her inside to see what she needed that late at night. Of course, Mara was cold like anybody who would come out of the snow, so she jumped on the bench by the stove to warm up a bit. Father was also warming up in the space where we usually stacked wood. Not wanting anybody to see him, he quietly told us children to sit in front of him to shield him. Fortunately, he was inconspicuous because our small petroleum lamps lit the room so poorly.

Mara wasted no time telling my mother the bad news. Partizans had come to our small place Brdo, which they visited only rarely. Mara said, "A message came for us to take food to the partizans." Mother asked if Mara's daughter-in-law Ana would take food to them from our family, and Mara agreed. She took bread, walnuts and

124

wine from us. We hoped that would be enough to satisfy them.

When Mara was gone, father became alert to possible unpleasantness. He got on the bed with one of us children as a shield, so that he would look like just another child. His premonition was right because not long after Mara had gone, there was another knock on the door. It was a soldier who asked mother if she could find space on her floor for his men to sleep. She explained that her old father-in-law coughed all night long, which wouldn't allow a good rest for those trying to sleep on the floor. Her explanation worked fine. The soldier left and didn't return. We weren't, however, free of them yet. Shortly another soldier came to ask if mother could accommodate some of their horses in our stall. Mother said that our stall was full of cattle, so there was no space for horses. She suggested that he go next door to our neighbors who had two stalls, and they left. We were finally free from further obligation, and by morning, the partizans had left. Father stayed in the house for a few days, but as he saw the need for preparation of wood to warm the house, he went to the edge of our yard and cut down one old walnut tree for fuel. By that time, of course, neighbors had seen him, so the whole neighborhood came to hear the story of how he had come home. He remained with us for one week, then went to our county office to turn himself in because they would have gotten him anyway, but if they came for him, they would punish him.

The war went on until that spring of 1945. After father left, we didn't hear anything about him. Was he alive or dead?

Chapter 7: **Two Kinds of Wolves**

In the spring of 1945, Grandfather Bosiljevac left us forever without knowing whether his son Janko had survived the war. I was nine years old when I found out that I did not have to take food to partizans and mother would not have to cook for them. World War II was over that spring, but we had no idea whether father was alive or dead. Everybody was happy the war was over, but for us there wasn't much of a change. Mother and we three little children were alone, working very hard to have something to eat through the entire year. Drago was eleven, but after grandpa died a man's responsibilities fell on his shoulders. He was the one who worked with the oxen, hauling crops home from the fields and bringing wood to warm our home in winter. Mother did the rest, running all the time from one job to another. After I grew up, I loved to try to do everything that the men were doing. It make me feel capable and strong, physically and mentally. Mother worked hard, but she was often afraid of the oxen. One was mean and chased people when he was free to run in the field. He even gave my brother a hard time, but Drago was able to handle him.

Although Drago kept busy with all of the farm work, he did find time to get away from his duties and visit his friends. When they came to our house, I participated in their games, but I never went to their yards because they were boys. Most of the time I worked with mother. I felt sorry for her alone in the field, so I kept her company, which made both of us feel better.

Shortly after the war ended, mother discovered that father was indeed alive, but he stayed in the army for the rest of the year, finally coming home that winter. Our lives had been hard without him, but it was hard after he came home, as well. Father was a good provider, making sure we had food on our table. If we had a bad year for crops, he found some way to buy food so that we wouldn't be hungry. But he was a strict disciplinarian, maybe more than he should have been. He wanted his home to function like clockwork, perhaps something he had learned in the army. He pushed us to work very hard, but he also  pushed himself. Mother was such a wonderful person. She didn't complain and she also overdid working, but she did protest when father pushed us children too hard.

(We sent this family picture to Uncle Marko In America.)

The summers after the war were dry and rainless, which meant greater hardship for all of us. In 1950, I went with other ladies to bring water from the same spring my mother had gone to in that hot summer of 1935, while she was pregnant with me. One year father and I had to go nineteen times with oxen and wagon to get water from Obrh Creek in the village of Ribnik. We went with many other people from the upper villages every other day to fill two barrels. Not only my generation and my parents' generation, but every generation before ours had to do the same when the dry seasons came.In spite of the dry weather, those years after father came home were happy ones for all of us. Father would play with us, although only for a short time. Then he would put on a serious face and say "Stop." We knew that meant we were not to disturb him anymore. Mother was so happy to have father home. They had been quite young when they married; they were still young as we became teenagers. When I was thirteen, mother was thirty-three and father was thirty-five. I remember that often they and we children were frequently like brothers and sisters rather than parents and children. Coming home from farming duties, mother prepared dinner while we children played in our yard. After we ate, if father was in a good mood we would sit on the porch and sing all together. He was a good singer, and we enjoyed making our own entertainment. I'm sure the neighbors could hear us clearly.

While grandma was alive she had forbidden mother to even come close to the stove. Had grandma been a good cook, mother wouldn't have minded, but my parents complained to grandma that she cooked too much food when it was plentiful and squeezed everything when it wasn't. Under grandma's domination, mother even had to care for us children as grandma told her to. My parents tried to avoid arguments with grandma. If father favored mother's position, everybody was in trouble. This was a common problem with young Croatian married couples who often suffered when living in the husband's family house. Daughters-in-law were considered outsiders, but they had to abide by the husband's parents' wishes in order to eventually inherit the property. Later in life I had to live that way with my husband's family, but fortunately for a much shorter time.

After grandma's death, mother was able to take over the kitchen on her own. Mother enjoyed making everything taste better. A very organized woman, she calculated all the food available and counted out equal proportions to last for the entire year. We ate the same amount every month, summer and winter. Mother heeded the old saying *"Cjela koza i sit vuk,"* (Save the goat and satisfy the wolf.)

Young couples today find it hard to relate to life as it was then in Europe. Now married couples usually have choices about how they will live. Those who do not work together can't get along and frequently divorce. Those who build a solid marriage are lucky. Hopefully, more husbands and wives will appreciate each other and develop strong, lasting families built on faith, understanding and hard work.

Our family had a difficult time under communism following the war, but tried to ignore political problems so we could have good times together once in awhile. Father enjoyed visiting his sister in Zagreb; he always took her and her daughter some "goodies" from our farm. These could include walnuts, wine, apples and whisky. As much as he loved to go there, we loved as much being free from his discipline for a time. When he was home, there was no jumping in the house, no excessive noise. Sometimes when we three children fought, we wanted Mom to be the judge and punish the guilty child. She didn't want to do that, and all she said was, "If you can't get along with each other, stay away." Drago was usually funny and wanted to show off with his freedom, so in his excitement he often ended up breaking something like a glass or a picture. Father usually had brought those things from aunt Dragica, and a drinking glass getting broken was a big deal. It was easy to buy one in the city, but not on the countryside, so if one broke, we feared father's reaction. Sometimes he stayed in Zagreb even a whole week, but when he got home he was usually in a good mood although feeling a little guilty over having had a small vacation while mother and the children had not. Father promised me many times to take me to Zagreb when the world exhibition occurred once a year, but that never happened.

During the war many things in our home had deteriorated, and after the war we couldn't afford to buy things from a store. Uncle Marko and Aunt Mary from Kansas City helped us, mostly with clothes and some money. For a few years after the war we could buy nothing because goods from our factories that were working were going somewhere else. People talked about how the communist government was sending things our factory produced to Russia in exchange for guns. Those who worked for the government received some kind of coupons instead of money. Sometimes they sold these coupons to others for money. We still had to make our own fabric, though, even ten years after the war. We also kept a few sheep for wool to knit into socks and sweaters.

Nobody had seen a wolf in our county till after the war, but in 1945 they appeared here and there in our forest. People said they had run away from the army in the Lika region, their traditional home. We children had always been afraid of wolves because of story books about them, but in real life, nobody had seen them in our area before. In the spring of 1945, however, we noticed the first signs of their presence. As my family owned only two sheep and two little twin lambs, Drago and other neighborhood boys were in the forest with the cattle while letting the sheep graze on young spring leaves and grass in a local pasture. As usual they had left the animals in the forest while they played games nearby. When they returned, they found my brother's little lamb dead, showing signs of a wolf's bite. No one had experienced such a thing before, and no one had seen the wolf, but no one had to. The damage was done, and all of us knew it would happen again. Sure enough, shortly another sheep was found killed, although again, no one saw the wolf.

During the fall of that year, mother and I were busy gathering dry fern while my brothers were with the cattle and sheep, not too far distant. Suddenly we heard young people yelling "Wolf, Wolf!" We thought the cry was just in play, so we continued to work. Mother drifted a little away downhill, and as I turned my head I spotted an unbelievable sight – a real, live wolf, about 300 feet away, stood staring at me! What would a ten-year-old girl think when a creature from her story books suddenly appeared in real life? Mother heard me scream and came toward me. The only thing I remembered was that some people said crying *"Peheir"* could drive a wolf away. I didn't know what it meant, but that is what I tried. He just stood there looking at me and I at him. Much larger than a German Shepherd, his eyes glowed a shiny yellow, his hair hung stiff and gray, and his presence totally devastated me. Deciding, apparently, that I was not a tasty sheep, he walked slowly back toward the forest and disappeared from view. Later somebody told us how that same creature had killed Peter Hrastovcak's sheep at the time mother and I had heard shepherds yelling "wolf." Drago said that same wolf chased sheep to the bottom of a valley, grabbing one and killing her before everyone's eyes, but when people began yelling, he left hungry. Luckily he hadn't attacked me when he arrived a few minutes later. Our area was not free of these creatures for some time, but that was the only time I ever met one face-to-face. Believe me, once was enough! More and more often they continued to prey on our sheep until it became impossible for us to keep the few that remained. They also attacked dogs right in our yards, usually at night. Once when we had a heavy snow the two Hrastovcak brothers saw a wolf on the edge of our village, coming closer and closer until the men took pitchforks in their hands and chased him back to the forest. When we came out of our home, he was gone, but we could see his trail clearly in the snow. Later, after the sheep had disappeared and hunters had chased the beasts from our area, they finally moved on. Nobody has seen them since.

Wolves were not the farmers' only problem, however. Drought hit us again, and some kind of bug began destroying what crops were left. Even our wheat vanished before it was ready for harvesting. People guessed that possibly soldiers had brought the insects, transferring them from one country to another. We had no spray of any kind to help get rid of these pests. Everything seemed bent on destroying our hard earned livelihood.

Shaggy grey animals weren't the only kind of 'wolves' to prey on us. Members of the communist regime didn't help us either. To the contrary, they were destroying us as well. We worked hard to recover from the war, but they imposed many unusual burdens on people in the countryside. On top of the already unfair taxes we were forced to pay on our land, whether or not there was any crop, they forced us to give them so many kilos of meat, corn, wheat, wine and lard. No one could cut off 50 kilos of meat from their cow to give them; therefore, two or three neighbors bought one cow and gave it to the government even if we ourselves were rarely able to eat meat.

Once a man named Josip Slak went from house to house collecting lard which we had been ordered to turn over to the government. He had a millhouse which did fine in rainy seasons, but when there was no rain, he had a hard time feeding his family, since his millhouse operated on water. He had searched for some kind of work, so the communists gave him the job of collecting lard. Josip was a nice man, so people understood why he had to do this job. Usually they offered him a little wine to drink while he was there. During the time the snow was heavy, he approached our property as we children were playing in the snow. He was walking somewhat strangely, then in a second he fell down in the snow and struggled to get up. He was pretty drunk already. All he could say was "masce, masce," which meant "lard." We helped him get up and took him to our house to collect lard from our family. When some real communist "wolves" came to Stjepan and Mara Bosiljevac to collect corn and meat, Mara tried with a pitchfork to stop them from entering her house. However, when the men pointed a gun at her, she ran to the house and they took meat from her attic where it was smoking.

We also had to give the communists free wood from our forests so they could build houses for those who had fought on their side in the war. Then the communists decided to build a new county government building. They ordered the people of the county to dig huge amounts of dirt from the ground and take it away with oxen and wagons, all, of course, without pay. Our people felt we had returned to slavery. Eventually the communists saw that the work was taking too much time, so they gave up on that idea. All that hard work had gone for nothing.

These conditions continued until 1948. When we fed partizans during the war, they had been satisfied with whatever we cooked for them as long as it was food, but the communists took whatever and however much they wanted without pay or even gratitude. We were pleased when that type of robbery ended, even if other forms of intimidation occurred.

In Ribnik County we had several families with at least one member who worked in the county office and, of course, had to be a communist. They terrorized those who did not agree with what they did. They must have known what misery they caused to poor individual families and could have protected us from their superiors, but they didn't. My father was appointed to represent people from Grice. When he and one more man participated in their county meetings, father defended our people who worked so hard on their small farms.

My father's duty was to go from house to house and write in his book how many head of cattle, pigs, and chickens they had and the quantity of crops grown so the communists could take a portion for themselves. Father walked home from that meeting with Drago Jarmek and one of the communists who had also attended. They were arguing because my father hadn't written in his book the correct number of pigs Mato Hadusek had. The communists already had spies in the villages who had given them information about what each family had. My father told the communist, Frank Jagas, "When I write in my book the things people have, I am not counting pigs or cows. I am just writing what they say to me." The argument became quite tense. Frank took a pistol from his pocket and put it close to my father's head. Drago tried to tell both of them to calm down and leave politics aside, so my father backed down. He saw that truth had no place in communism. These human "wolves' were devouring our way of life and for some of our people, our values, as well.

Several years later, Frank was fired from his communist post. They didn't need men like him with no education; they needed them only for dirty work. I witnessed my father's accidental encounter with Frank after Frank had lost his job. It was in our forest when we came to cut some wood to bring home. Frank, who was working just like everybody else, had come to cut wood with his brother. As my father came closer to them, Frank disappeared behind some bushes. My father talked with Frank's brother, who had never been happy with what Frank was doing. He never knew, perhaps, that his brother had almost killed my father.

To the communists, everyone was either *"druze"* or *"drugarica,"* both of which meant "comrade." Even a husband should be druze and his wife drugarica. Once Izidore Car was working in his yard when communists came and asked, "Where is your drugarica?" Izidore was upset and answered, "She is not my drugarica, she is my wife." That comment caused Izidore to sit in jail for six months.

Even when we were small and later young adults, we witnessed, then remembered, hundreds of unusual occurrences during the communist regime. The worst ones involved their luring young people into their lair by promising a job or free schooling. Participation in their meetings was important. That was where they promised everything under the sun to party members. They praised all their own accomplishments and insulted all capitalistic ones. Some people accepted the empty promises, but others believed nothing they said, whether the statements were true or false.

As children we continued our basic education through the fourth grade, which was all our parents could afford for us. When we finished, we could read, write, and perform basic math, and before 1945 we learned some of our Croatian history. After the war, though, we learned only Yugoslavian and communistic versions of education. During the war Croatia functioned independently, so when I attended first and second grades we had a priest to handle our religious instruction. Afterwards, our "education" consisted of communist songs, war, Yugoslav president Tito's accomplishments, and communistic philosophy, though our parents never approved. When we told our parents what we were being taught, they had to teach us the truth in their own way – to believe in God, as we were learning in school not to believe.

After the war the communists did at least give children the opportunity for free higher education, but our parents didn't want the communists to force their ideas on our minds. They were right, but we didn't get ahead as some young people did. I had lots of dreams about doing things my way and going where I would like, but I couldn't without my parents' permission. They still thought that it was not a good idea for young girls to be in the city. I thought at least I could get some kind of work in the city, even if it paid only small wages, but my parents expected a better situation in the future.

I was also afraid to get married in the country and live the type of life my mother and many other ladies were living.   I heard them complain about life with their husbands' parents. In-laws usually looked at the girls as outsiders, not as someone who had married their sons. A few women like Grandma Magdalena Jagas understood this fully and had good relationships with their sons' wives. They understood that if they loved their sons' wives, their sons' love would also always be theirs.

Before, during and after World War II, life over there was hard and inconvenient, but we had some things which were much better than they are today. We lived a simple life without fear of losing our children in car accidents or being victims of widespread fraud as exists around the world now. Places like that where I lived have disappeared, and livable cities have now become huge, impersonal metropolises.   We lived in a breathtaking, breathable environment all year long. It was unpolluted and healthful. The life that came after the war didn't fit everyone, although some people chose it anyway. Jobs were available in communist factories, but the party pressed people to join, especially if they had educated them free. Some young people were forced to go get jobs in cities because their small farms and large families couldn't sustain them.

In the late 40's I was a teenager who was already thinking about my future and, of course, my married life if that should happen. I liked many of the boys in our area, who were nice to me and handsome, too, but I got chills observing how many of our women were treated by their in-laws after marriage. Although my father was strict, he respected his children, so I couldn't imagine being trapped in a husband's family where I would be a "second fiddle."

At age fourteen I reached my full height of 5'5" but was skinny, which made me somewhat uncomfortable in the company of other girls. Finally my body began filling out. We girls never could go alone with boys during nighttime. We went to dances together and returned home in the same group of boys and girls. Father was strict with me and my brothers about attending dances or other teenage activities, but mother wanted us to go. She had to argue constantly with father to get us permission. In Brdo, the only other girl was Ana Hrastovcak, who, although she was six years older than I, was wonderful and helped me get over my shyness. The girls I had gone to school with were scattered all over Grice and Veselice. Without telephones, it was difficult to get together with them.

When I reached the age of sixteen I began to have a good time with both male and female friends. I didn't even think of having one boyfriend; I just wanted to be everybody's friend, free to dance, joke and laugh with them. We were like brothers and sisters, most of us within two or three years of the same age.

There was one boy, Janko Horvat, who was older and more mature than the rest. He had been in the army where he had learned discipline. He became a protector for us girls. When younger boys said something inappropriate to us, he would turn to them saying, "I don't want to hear that kind of word being said to our girls." If we were walking together to or from a dance, one boy might use an embarrassing word to another boy, and Janko would remind them, "Don't you see our girls could hear you? We are not alone." When we went to a dance in neighboring Netretic County, our boys wanted to dance with girls from there or even with some girls from Karlovac, but Janko ordered them to dance with us first; then later on they could dance with anyone they wanted to. Janko also asked them to watch to see if we were dancing or not. If we were not, then he asked our boys to dance with us so we would not be standing there alone. Sometimes Janko's subtle "suggestions" worked, and sometimes not.

Today, young people believe in fast love and don't look farther down the road to think how that marriage would work for life. Our marriages had to be planned carefully because divorce was rare, and married couples usually lived together forever. We knew not to get too involved with a young man until our parents would allow us to get married. If we didn't have their permission, we might not have a place to live in their house and on their farm. Most of us didn't want to marry someone only to satisfy our parents, but neither did we want to alienate them with our defiance.

Janko Horvat felt he could not marry a girl from Grice because he was one of nine children; therefore, he couldn't be the only one to bring a wife to his parents' house. In another county he married a girl who was an only child, and they lived in her mother's house on her small farm. This type of thing happened frequently. Love wasn't the only consideration; it was what would make a couple's lives fit better that had to be considered.

Chapter 8: **Marriage and Escape**

When my parents and grandparents were young, girls often married as early as fifteen years of age, but during my youth that shifted a little higher. My friends were married at the age of eighteen or more. When I was seventeen, I began weighing my freedom against the possibility of marriage. For the first time I was enjoying being in control of myself. My father had been strict, and I didn't want to marry a man who would have the same control of me.

My freedom, however, didn't last as long as I had planned. When I was 17½ years old, a young man named Ivan Jarmek came back into my life. After working in Karlovac for two years, he had joined the army, serving in aviation, and completed his service in just under three years, from 1950-1953. He was born and grew up in Grice, in a place nicknamed Jarmek's Valley, only ten-minutes walking distance from Brdo. I was friends with his sister and other girls from Jarmek's Valley, but, because he was five years older, I hadn't talked much with Ivan prior to his arrival home from the military.

I had been aware that he was known to have an arrogant personality, but I discovered he was really two persons in one – arrogant when he wanted to be, but nice and kind when he felt like it. I never thought he would ever say a word to me because of my shy nature, but now we saw something in each other that we liked. We were two different people, but he was one of the nicest looking young men in our area, so I thought our personalities might come together little by little. It did bother me when he threw arrogant remarks at me sometimes, but then he would try to smooth up what he had said.

At dances that spring and summer, he would ask me to dance with him, but I backed off somewhat. I tried never to hurt anyone's feelings with smart remarks, so I did not appreciate them from Ivan. My character is like both my parents: I am as soft as my mother and as tough as my father. Ivan's looks and his maturity appealed to me, but he still had a lot to learn if he wanted to become involved with me. I learned a lot about him, too. As we became acquainted in the months that followed, I discovered that he had a softer side, nothing like the one he showed me at first.

In the summer of 1953, Ivan asked me to marry him without knowing how our parents could prepare for a fall wedding. Our tradition involved marrying in the fall, when food and wine is plentiful and farm work is over for the season. It was hard for me to imagine being trapped by going steady with one boy and plan to marry him and settle down. I had heard many stories from girls who dated one man for a long period of time only to have their family change their minds and decide that the daughter or the son should marry someone else. My fears nearly came to reality. After Ivan and I had been going together for more than a year, our love had grown, but the atmosphere in his family toward me had changed, and that wasn't at all what I wanted in my marriage.

Despite his parents' reservations, Ivan's and my marriage did take place on January 8, 1955. That day the weather was icy over the snow, so travel with horse and wagon would be difficult, but that is what we did. When Ivan and his party came to pick me up for the wedding, he had forgotten a ring. I wanted to send my brother to get it, but cousin Ljubica Bretz offered me her ring for the ceremony, so that is what I used. At that time our county office was on the second floor in Ribnik Castle. My maid of honor should have been my cousin Zdenka Savor, who lived in Karlovac with her mother and younger sister Ruzica. Unfortunately, they couldn't come because of the ice, so cousin Ana Maver was my maid of honor, although being only fifteen years old, she couldn't be my witness. After a discussion, the county clerk, Mika Tomasic, signed the certificate. We were married not by a judge but by a county clerk. Under communism, that document was legal. From the county office we then went to church, where we were married by a priest.

According to our tradition, the reception went on for twenty-four hours, beginning some time after noon. Now it seems silly to me, but nobody wanted to be the first to break this custom. The ladies from my side followed a wagon full of bedroom furniture to Ivan's house and arranged it in the bedroom for us. They stayed with guests from Ivan's side, eating, drinking and dancing until midnight. Then they all came to our house together for Ivan to claim me and take me to his home . . . but not before everyone ate, drank and danced over and over until late afternoon.

Finally, everything was ready. A young man carrying the flag led the procession. He was followed by musicians playing music all the way. *(Fortunately, in our case, the trip was short. Sometimes, if the bride came from a distant village, the trip could take a long time.)* Ivan and I rode in the wagon, followed by all of the guests. When we arrived at my new home, I changed from bridal white to traditional clothing. Although everybody was tired by then, the eating and drinking resumed until far into the night. Finally the guests disappeared little by little.

Before Ivan and I married, we had developed a secret plan. Nobody knew about it, not even those in our families. We only hoped that it could become reality later in our lives. So I began my new life in my husband's family house on January 10, 1955, on my mother's 40th birthday. I regretted my situation had to be like that, but over time I came to believe that everything that happened to me happened for a reason – a reason that would bring Ivan and me to America some years later.

We began our new life together. It was no different than the type of life many other young couples lived in our countryside, with the husband's parents and other members of his family. We knew that this would be temporary for us, but we didn't know how long it was going to be that way. Ivan had worked previously in Karlovac and could probably get his old job there again. I asked Ivan about that possibility, and for the first time, he started to explain: "You probably will never fully understand how much I want to get an education in some kind of trade. When I worked in the Yugoturbina factory I applied for this training, but when I came to the office for my interview, the communists asked me to join the communist party, to give up religion and my Croatian nationality, and to sign an agreement to give them a portion of my payroll loan for ten years." I asked Ivan if anybody had agreed to that kind of demand. "Yes," he replied. "Many did that to get ahead, but I couldn't, and I knew my father wouldn't allow it even if I wanted to." When Ivan refused to sign permission for these restrictions, he had no choice but to join the army.

So, now our lives went on as before for a year and six months. Ivan was constantly thinking about our little secret, but didn't discuss it with me again. During May of 1956, however, Ivan's friend Drago Secen came home from the army. He told Ivan that during his military service he had been stationed on the Austrian-Yugoslav border. That triggered an idea in Ivan's mind. If Drago thought the same as Ivan, Drago's knowledge of that border area could give them a way out. Now Ivan began to share with me a discussion about our secret and his plan. He needed for me to agree to it. Finally we decided that he and Drago would leave illegally and cross to Austria, just as many other young people had done. It was too early to attempt this. They needed a very good way to get across the border, which wasn't as safe as they had thought.

Ivan and his friend had not planned their trip as carefully, perhaps, as they should have, but when they decided the time was right, Ivan and Drago left one night, not completely certain how to find the road out of the country. Leaving me behind, they took that risk feeling that whatever would happen would happen. That was one of the most painful days in my life. I don't even remember what I did and what I thought that day. I only waited for some kind of news. Did they succeed or didn't they? I wandered around Ivan's family's house like a lost sheep who doesn't know where her flock is. I just spent the long hours waiting for news – good or bad. I don't remember whether it came the next day or the third, but it was horrible. I heard that somebody saw Ivan and Drago in Karlovac, where police were taking them to jail. In democratic countries, people are taken to jail because they are criminals, but in communist countries people are often sent to jail not because they hurt someone or because they stole something, but only because they wanted to advance their lives in freedom, without the label of being a communist party member.

I didn't want to believe the news, but I ran for comfort to my parents' home. It turned out not to be news to them. My father had hurried to see Ivan in Karlovac as soon as he heard. This is reality, I thought. The worst is really happening to Ivan and me. The next day I went to see Ivan, but we couldn't talk about how he and Drago had been caught. Both Ivan and Drago were sentenced to five months in jail, and Ivan got an additional three months because some people didn't like that we weren't communist sympathizers.

Even a friend could be turned by the communists, and Juro Secen had once been Ivan's friend and Drago's closest neighbor. After the war he had gotten a job as a salesman in a clothing store in Karlovac. Because even the stores were under communist control, some people suspected that Juro was more than a salesman. Unfortunately, my husband and his companion had to find out the truth of that suspicion the hard way.

Ivan and his friend had gone to Karlovac where they boarded the train for Zagreb. On the train they saw their friend and former neighbor, but didn't talk to him. In Zagreb they had planned to go to Maribor, Slovenia, and walk to the Austrian border from there. But they saw Juro Secen again in Zagreb, and he saw them. If they had realized he was spying on them, they could have done some shopping and then returned home, but they thought Juro was a better person than he was. So, when they arrived in Maribor, two police stopped them, identified them, and soon were on their way to jail.

All these years later I am still upset over Juro Secen's betrayal (even though he is in his grave), because he was once Ivan's friend. God certainly didn't reward him for his dirty work: even the communists got rid of him when he lost one of his legs and wasn't of use to them anymore. Ivan and Drago, on the other hand, would go on to live productive lives – Ivan in Kansas City and Drago in Toronto, Canada.

Back in 1951, before I married Ivan, my father had gone to Zagreb to see his sister. While he was there, he visited the American embassy where he registered me for the quota to enter America. Had that number ever have come to the top, I could have come legally to my uncle and his family. At the time, it was more like a joke, and all of us had forgotten it. In my future, however, something would happen, although it would be, by then, too late for Ivan and me.

Ivan completed his eight months of jail time on February 2, 1957, so we continued living with his family. Winter crept by as usual, until the gorgeous spring arrived. Fruit trees put out lively blooms. Birds arrived to sing to us in the early mornings and continuing through the days. The beauty of nature had always made me happy before, but not that spring. Ivan and I just waited for something good to happen, although we had no idea what. Because one chance for us had failed in Maribor, we wouldn't abandon our plan forever; in fact, we had more reason now to get out of the country because we were now more hated and suspected by the communists.

Thursday, June 20, 1957, was our Catholic holiday, Corpus Christi *(Tijelovo)*. We had a special noon mass in our church on every holy day. So this day I walked with other ladies about one hour to church and one back. Nothing seemed different until I returned home. As usual, I went to my room first to exchange my shiny clothes for more appropriate ones. As I was changing, Ivan came into our room. I knew as soon as I saw him that he had something important to tell me. Ivan can't hide his feelings ever, but by then I could read him well, and I could tell something had made him frightened. "What is it?" I asked, but it was some time before he could speak: "Tonight we have the opportunity to go to Italy." "To Italy?" I stammered. We had never favored going there; our plan had always been to go to Austria. Ivan explained in detail how that plan would work and who would take us there, because we would need more than one agent. My parents had quite a bit of money saved until Ivan and I would need it. Surely a better future would be reason enough. This decision created quite a lot of pressure for us inexperienced young people.

When we decided to go, I ran to my parents to ask for advice and money. Since it was a holiday, I found only my mother in the back yard. She was drying some freshly cut grass while she enjoyed the sun. Father had taken off with friends, and Jure was in Zagreb to take a physical exam for the Yugoslav army. Although it was difficult for me to tell her the reason for my visit, I explained everything and asked her for two things, advice and money. She replied, "Father and I would give you one of your requests – that will be the money – but advice we won't. This has to be only Ivan's and your decision." That message was certainly honest enough to take to Ivan. "If we do decide to leave," I said, "we will come this evening to your home to get the

148

money and say goodbye. I hope father and Jure will see us before we leave in these circumstances."

On June 20, 1957, we set off on the most difficult voyage of our lives. I packed a few pieces of clothing for Ivan and me. We were to wait till darkness when neighbors wouldn't see us leaving. I left first, going to my parents. Ivan came a little later to pick up the money and me. Leaving home as if I were coming back the next day, I didn't even get to say goodbye to my brothers; Jure hadn't returned from Zagreb before we left, and Drago was somewhere on the Adriatic Sea with the navy. I don't even remember what I was thinking. I had no idea what our future was going to look like, nor where it would be. I left that to Ivan.

A few small steps toward realizing our secret dream of America had begun. We walked through the forest to meet our first contact in the village of Bogovci. There we met our first agent, Josep Kucenic, and Miha Trzok, who was traveling with us to Italy for the same reason as we were. We walked together down to the millhouse owned by Miha's family on the Kupa River. They had a small boat in which we crossed the river during the night. In Slovenia, a highway led us to a little place named Crnomalj. When we came close, we crossed a creek on a small, enchanting bridge. Miha and Josip, the man who would take us to the main leader, bent down close to the water, watching small fish swimming in the clear water. For a minute they forgot what kind of trip we were making, where danger threatened every minute. Ivan brought them back to reality, "How come fish are on your minds when police could catch us any time?" They snapped out of their reverie at that, and we continued our journey to the railroad station in Crnomalj, arriving in the morning of June 21st.

This was my first experience traveling with Ivan on a dangerous trip. For him, though, this was the second time, and he was unbelievably frightened of ending up in jail again. In the station's small waiting room were a few tables and chairs where we sat and waited for the train. The men each drank a beer on their empty stomachs, but I couldn't drink anything. I would rather have eaten if possible, but there was no food available. We waited as if for a verdict in a trial rather than a happy trip, especially Ivan. When Miha noticed how depressed his new friend felt, he tried to make his nervousness less noticeable by saying, "Hey, Ivan, is that tooth giving you pain again?" Ivan replied, "It is hurting like hell!" I almost laughed because I knew he was in pain, but pain of an entirely different kind.

Fortunately, we didn't have to wait too long for a train. With nothing else to do, I looked out the window at the passing scenery. Ivan, however, had his mind occupied with possible dangers. He looked every person over, assessing them and deciding if any were looking at us. He didn't say anything to me until a young soldier stepped onto the train at one of the stops. Turning to me, he asked, "See that soldier – how he looked at us? I am afraid he could be looking for people like us who are on the way out of the country." "Don't look at him," I said, "Look out the window as I am, and nothing will happen." Of course, the soldier frightened me, too, but luckily he got off at the following stop, which let Ivan and me breathe a little bit easier. We got to Ljubljana without trouble, where we met the person who would take us to the Italian border. Josep, who had brought us to this point, returned home to Bogovci.

Our contact from this point was a lady whose husband was waiting in his apartment with two of their children. The apartment was not far from the Italian border, in the small city of Goricia, but we were still far from reaching that place, and anything might happen on the way. Ivan and Miha were sitting together, and the lady and I had another seat. Once I stepped out on the car's platform where a young man asked me where I was going. I was quite concerned about what I should say until I remembered my little brother Jure telling me of a school trip to a cave in Postojna. So I said, "I am going to Postojna to see a cave my brother told me was very interesting." He wanted to talk to me longer, but I was busy thinking how to get rid of him.

We continued traveling past stately evergreens on the way to Italy, but at an intersection where a sign pointed one way to Postojna Cave and another to Goricia we got off the train. Our leader knew that spot well. She had us sit on a beautiful terrace of a restaurant by that intersection. "I am going to visit my sister on one of those streets," she said. "Then, when I return we will get on the bus right at this intersection." So there was nothing for us to do but take something to drink, although none of us had eaten for the entire day, and it was then mid afternoon.

We couldn't help but realize that she had left with our money. Could we trust her? Will she return to take us with her or will she just disappear? Well, there was nothing for us to do but wait, and wait, and wait . . . Finally Ivan's nerves snapped. Turning to Miha and me, he said, "Let's go home before the police find us and take us to jail." Well, it did look as if the lady was looking out for her own safety and not for ours. My body tingled thinking of returning without our money. Perhaps our neighbors already knew where we had gone. Miha and I didn't want to turn back, so I said, "I am going down the street. Maybe I will meet her someplace." I started off, but after going about 200 feet I met her. I said, "We are concerned that you were not coming for such a long time," but she replied, "A bus will be here soon, so I am here now to be ready for the trip with you to my home."

It was close to dark when we departed from that intersection, but when we arrived at the bus stop, her husband and two children were waiting for us. Then it looked as if we were their friends, not just some people they had never seen before. Ivan took one child by the hand and Miha took the other. The couple's home was not too far from the Italian border, but I was so tired by that time I didn't care where I was going or what might happen.

We were now so close to Italy but still so far from realizing our dream that I really, really couldn't concentrate on our situation. I knew only that I was tired and hungry, so I left everything else to Ivan and Miha. The lady gave me some cookies and let me lie on her bed to rest. The time for us to cross the border was set for 1:00 a.m. on June 22. I lay on that bed, falling asleep in an instant. While I slept, Toni took Ivan and Miha to see the place where we were to cross the border and to give them instructions on how to do it. This hurdle, in the center of the city of Goricia, was crucial to our success.

The lady came to wake me when it was time for us to leave. As we left the apartment, Toni told us that he had arranged with someone to let us cross that border during the full lighting in the center city. Otherwise, he said, not even a mouse could cross that fence. The three-foot fence sat on a two-foot high concrete wall, making the height about the same as my 5'5". That worried me, so I tried to tell Ivan to jump across, then let me hand him our things and jump after him. Miha was already on the other side. Before I could say that, Ivan grabbed me around my waist, and I found myself on the other side of the fence, with bloody hands and a torn dress. Then Ivan jumped over. Both Ivan and Miha had grabbed a pole on the fence to help themselves, but I was so surprised when Ivan grabbed me that I had clutched the barbed wire fencing instead.

We were on the other side! That moment on the west side of the Iron Curtain, I thought to myself, "I have jumped into heaven!" America was still far in our future, but we had avoided falling into communist hands and sitting in their jails. Our future had a chance at last. It had been fifty years since my grandfather had arrived on Ellis Island. It had taken him three weeks on a ship from Trieste to America. It would take Ivan and me much longer than that, but we could not realize that then.

Now, on the western side of the fence, an Italian policeman approached us with a little smile on his face, saying something to us like, "You made it." He took us into their station where he and his buddies smiled to make us feel at ease after the ordeal we had just gone through. Seeing my bloody hands, one of the police reached in a cabinet for a bottle of whisky and compassionately cleaned my wounds, shaking his head over the sad, torn state of my dress. Since the hotel had been closed at midnight, we stayed in the station, which had three rooms. They tried to apologize about having us sleep there. They couldn't know that after one day and two nights without eating or sleeping, this was fine for us. They showed us to a room, saying to me that they would leave the door to Ivan's and my room open so I will not be frightened. I really wasn't frightened now. Besides, I was so tired that the jail room and bed were fine for me.

In the morning we had to complete our documents, but close to noon we had visitors from that hotel where we were supposed to stay later that day. Those visitors, two young men named Toni Mrvunac and Josip Pozeg, had come to see if anybody from their village had arrived. Miha Trzok was Toni's cousin, but Ivan and I didn't know either of them. That didn't matter; from that moment on we were friends. They returned to the hotel and brought food for us – our first in three days.

When our documents were completed we were free to go to the hotel. All the guests there were people from Yugoslavia who were on the same road as ours. Most were young people, many from the Slovenian

Federation and Croatia. We were free to tour the city of Goricia as we pleased, so we did. We went to the little Foce River, where some young people were swimming in clean but fast and dangerous water. One of the Slovenian girls named Maria was swimming there with others, mostly young boys, when she got in trouble in the fast water. She almost drowned, but Toni Mrvunac, who had learned to swim in the Kupa, saved Maria. We weren't good swimmers ourselves, but we enjoyed watching others swim.

I was tired of taking care of my long hair and wanted to get it short like all the other girls in that hotel. Toni took me to see a young lady named Maria at her beauty salon. I told her I wanted to get my hair cut and have a permanent. She tried hard to persuade me not to get the permanent, and I found out later how that process could ruin healthy hair like mine. When she found me to be persistent, Maria said, "I will cut it, but at least take some of the hair with you as a souvenir." But I insisted, "No, you keep it if you like." She probably sold it later on. Perhaps I should have listened to her. My hair is still thick, and it is easier to manage, but it never again has looked as healthy.

I was 21 years old at that time. Maria was somewhat older and single, so she liked our friend Toni and she tried to do some nice things for me. She took me shopping, where I bought a nice dress. We also went to a circus in that city, the only time I had ever seen one, and she gave me a broach shaped like an elephant. I had it for a long time, but lost it after we moved so often.

There was more to see in Goricia. The small, lovely city was nestled among high mountains. One of them stood on the Italian-Yugoslav border, facing Italy. The Yugoslav communists, who did everything to promote President Tito's image, painted his name in giant letters on the face of that mountain, perhaps to irritate the Italians.

Our hotel was fine for a vacation, but Ivan and I became bored without something useful to do. Both of us were constantly wondering what would be next for us. Also, Ivan wasn't at ease about being so close to the Yugoslav border, and he was anxious to leave Goricia.

So, on July 7th, sixteen days after we had crossed the border, we were headed west to a small city named Cremona. It was a hot day for a train ride from early morning to mid afternoon. First we traveled through mountainsides, then through flat land full of wheat and vineyards, arriving in Cremona in late afternoon. Being naïve, I expected another nice hotel, but instead, we were accommodated in a large army complex facility with about 800 people, mostly young, from all over Yugoslavia. We refugees were of all types of professions – doctors, teachers, priests and farmers – mostly young. All of us were desperate to start our lives over, using and developing our abilities in a free world. The communists had wasted many smart minds by forbidding people to develop their own businesses. Many of us were intelligent and skillful, but first we needed to learn other languages, then understand the profession, and eventually start our own businesses. We knew that the way ahead would not be simple, but nothing is too hard for a person who is determined and energetic. It was sad that so many of us who could have helped the deteriorated economies of Croatia and other Yugoslav states had to leave our homelands to accomplish something in life. We found many people in our complex who planned to immigrate to Australia, Canada or South America, but we had left our home for the dream of life in America, which was harder to enter.

At the complex in Cremona, unmarried people were housed in large halls where they had single beds stacked on top of each other, with females in separate halls from males. Married couples were accommodated in smaller rooms, with at least two families to a room. Ivan and I stayed in a room with another Slovenian couple who had an eleven-month-old son and another baby on the way. Couples like these, we saw later, had a hard time taking care of young children under these circumstances. Ten men were stacked in the next room, nine Slovenians and one Croatian. We became more like family than merely good neighbors.

We did search for old friends there. Ivan found one among the men, a young Slovenian named Josip. He had jumped the partition between our two rooms to talk with Ivan. He became a friend to Ivan, like the brother he had never had, and to me also. When Josip left the complex, we accompanied him to a bus, all three of us crying. Not all of those next door were completely honest like Josip. The only Croatian next door, Peter, also jumped the wall between us to talk to us. Although he had an unpleasant personality, he could be kind. Once I had hung my towel on the window to dry. It fell down in the courtyard, which was fenced with no exit in or out. Peter noticed I was upset because we had very little money to buy things, so he volunteered to get the towel, even though it was dangerous.

My only souvenir from that enchanting city is a snapshot we took in the park with friends. I was wearing that nice dress which I had bought in Goricia. The snapshot shows: standing, Ivan, me, and Toni Mravunac, whose final destination would be Kansas City; kneeling, Josip Pozeg with Vlado Suljada, both of whom now live in Canada – Josip in London and Vlado in Hamilton.

Three weeks after we arrived in Italy, Josep and Milka Krznaric joined us in Cremona. Milka is Toni Mravunac's sister. More and more people began arriving from our own county and parish.

We kept hoping that others from Grice would arrive, and finally Miho Jarmek came with his girlfriend, Kata Novosel. Miho had grown up in the same neighborhood as Ivan, and Kata and I had attended the same schools. Miho, who had been a cook in the Yugoslav Army, used this advantage to get a job in the camp kitchen. He and Kata wanted to get married in Cremona, so they arranged it with the court there. Ivan served as Miho's best man. We had hoped that we could travel together from Italy because the newlyweds wanted to immigrate to Canada. This didn't work out, however, so they ended up going to Venezuela, South America. We heard later that their lives there weren't that good.

We discovered that it would be difficult to emigrate from Italy to America. Other people who were on their way to America discussed with us how they had waited for months, some for more than a year, but were still in the Italian camps. Many Croatians decided to go to Australia, but we didn't want to do that. "I don't want to be without a job for so long, waiting for America to open the door for us," Ivan said, "I need to work."

Everybody had to be in the camps until they could get their first documents. This usually took about three months. They then would move on, either to another country or to a larger camp, like Brindizi or Bari in southern Italy. Some of our friends were sent there in order to enter France, but Ivan and I were still waiting in Cremona.

Meanwhile we did some rather boring things in that small city. There was a large hall on campus where for the first time in our lives we were able to watch television. We had a laundry facility in the camp where

157

we ladies washed and ironed for our families and sometimes for other men who asked for our help. Once the police were called to make peace between two agitated ladies who were arguing because only four irons were available for use by hundreds of us. A mean looking policeman with a heavy dark moustache found one of the ladies guilty of causing the disturbance. I felt sorry for that lady, although she really was guilty, because he told her that the authorities would send her back to Yugoslavia. She cried until the tears dripped down her face for all to see. Observing her reaction, he came near her. He said nothing, but took his handkerchief out of his pocket and wiped the tears from her face. All of us were surprised and pleased when she got to stay in Italy instead of being deported. I felt then that the Italians were softhearted and kind, and I came to like them for that. One would think they would be mean to the large crowd in that place, but they proved to be just the opposite.

All of us were free to go wherever we pleased in Cremona. Some might think we would have made trouble, perhaps stealing something because we needed everything. That was not the case. We created no disturbances in that city. We just loved to sightsee while we were there. Every one of us had left our homes to accomplish something, and we knew very well that we could do that only with honesty, hard work and dedication.

Down in a courtyard, a Catholic priest served mass every Sunday. Some of us participated, others didn't. We also had showers, with time arranged for ladies together. At first I was reluctant to shower with others, but I got used to it. It was hardest to wait in line three times a day for meals. At first Ivan and I waited together, but when he became bored he asked me to bring food for both us, so I did. (That is the story of my life – what Ivan liked to do he did, and what he didn't like he didn't do. . . so I did that, too.)

One time when both of us were waiting in line, a young Slovenian named Franc Cokel started a conversation. Ivan, who had nothing on his mind but getting a paying job, said, "I wish there were something to do here for money." Franc and his Slovenian buddies worked, but his friends were leaving for France in a few days. Franc pointed out to Ivan how he had this chance to work but he would need a partner for that job, which was to take charcoal to the second and third floors, where people used it to warm their houses in winter. Franc was always a happy, bubbling person, just the opposite of Ivan, but they were pulled together by this need to work and they continued their conversation. Both men were good natured and even tempered which made them friends from then on. When Ivan stopped standing in line, Franc and I talked every day and the three of us became friends. Ivan was happy to have found work, and he and Franc could then afford to go out in the evening to coffee shops to drink and watch television. They invited me to go with them, but I thought of our future when we would need money and usually didn't go with them. While the men were out I found ladies with whom I spent time, and I was usually busy washing and ironing for us two and Franc, and later for Franc's father.

From outside a theater, Ivan, Franc and I once saw a movie which showed black people from Africa. I had never seen them before, in life or in the movies.

One older lady, Kata Francic, had come from the village of Kunice, just across the forest from Grice. She later immigrated to Canada. The two of us went to church together in the evening and spent other time there, as well. The priest gave us a prayer book in the Croatian language, which I still have. Other ladies and I enjoyed many simple outings in that city. We went to the beautiful cathedral more than once, and we discovered a pleasant park where we could sit and breathe air from the mountain on one side and the ocean on another. Neither was too close to the park, but those special scents traveled far enough to reach Cremona. We walked the city streets, admiring the gorgeously stylish dresses of Italian ladies. We had only a few main pieces of clothing, which looked nothing like those, although I did have the one nice dress I had bought in Goricia.

We had to wait at least two long months to pass the Italians' inquiry. They researched whether we had criminal records or were connected to any communist organization. Finally we heard that they would send us down to southern Italy, which would leave us farther from the countries to which we wanted to go. This didn't fit our secret plan, so we had to make other plans – and fast. Although Franc's constant laughing and joking sometimes made me tired, we did need him because he spoke Italian. He needed us, too, because we helped him in other ways. One day Mario, a Slovenian friend of Franc's, was ready to leave for France. Before he left, Franc asked him to send information back to us on how and where he and his friends were crossing the border. Mario sent us the information, including a little map. With that information, we prepared for yet another uncertain voyage. We asked our neighbors, Miho Jarmek and his wife Kata, if they would like to come with us, but they refused, still hoping to immigrate to Canada. They expected Ivan's aunt Lojza Novosel, who was also their relative, would sign papers for them. For some reason she didn't do it, so they had to go to Venezuela. We hoped that we could work in France and wait there to find haven somewhere else, hopefully America.

We prepared two pieces of luggage, one for each of us, and said goodbye to Cremona, but to nobody else. That trip was again a secret, for we had no papers with which to travel. We hoped we were going closer to America, but we were uncertain when we might arrive and what we would have to go through before our plan could become a reality.

Chapter 9: **Our Unusual Route to America**

Early in the morning of September 16, 1957, four of us exited a large door which was usually guarded. We left without luggage so we would not be questioned, but some friends then lowered our bags through the window to us. The Italian police might have suspected what was happening, but they didn't stop us because we weren't Italian citizens.

Four of us – Ivan and I and Franc and his father, went to the bus stop where we ordered coffee. We were naïve enough to start on that trip without even a donut. We probably thought we would get to France much faster than we did. Ivan and Franc organized everything; Franc's father and I knew nothing, not even where the French border was. The only map we had was one Franc's friend had sent us, just one little piece of paper that I didn't even understand.

I was sick on the bus because my stomach was empty, and it became worse when we reached the oceanside where the bus traveled a winding road. *(Twenty-nine years later we would travel the same route, and I expected the same highway. However, by then a new highway had been built; the ride was smoother, but we missed the sights we had seen before on that beautiful Italian coast.)*

We were traveling without documents and were afraid of having police check us for papers. Had they found us out they perhaps would have sent us back, either to Italy or to Yugoslavia. We were lucky and arrived by afternoon to Ventimiglia, a city closest to the French border. We needed to decide now, which direction do we turn? Which way is the French border? How far are we from it? Well, we were close to the ocean on the south, but we knew enough to avoid that highway which would lead to a police checkpoint at the French border. So we turned north on a smaller road that led between the Alps. We knew this was not the way we should go. As we walked through a residential area, we saw a heavy rain sliding down the mountain toward us. We should find shelter quickly to prevent being soaked to the skin. Franc ran to one house where people stood on their porch and asked them if they had umbrellas we could buy, but they did not. We didn't expect them to, but we hoped they would invite us under their roof. They did not. Perhaps they were afraid of strangers. The rain lasted just long enough for us to get really wet, but we walked away from the area while Ivan and Franc consulted that small map. We knew we needed to head west, but on which road? There were two, one led to the mountains or between them and the other wound up to a smaller hill. We took the left one to that hill, walking on a nice paved road as the sunset closed in on us.

Turning north away from houses, we searched for a safe place to spend the night. We found a small dip which looked like a plate. Clear of any brush, it had only an olive tree under which we stretched out and tried to sleep. I couldn't because the night was so chilly. We waited anxiously for daylight to warm us up. When morning came, we saw new snow on those Alps north of us, which accounted for the frigid air. To the south we saw the ocean, and on the east that little city where we had gotten off the bus. Yes, we did see the west, but we didn't like the kind of west we were seeing. We had dreamed of the French border right on that hill where we had spent the night.

We found ourselves, we thought, still in Italy with no idea how close the French border might be. Turning away from houses we slid down from the hill, but found ourselves in blackberry bushes which stopped us. We went back up the hill and decided we must do something we had tried to avoid – we had to ask people for advice.

We stopped at an enchanting little house where we saw an older man and a younger lady sitting at a small table. Franc asked her in Italian where the French border was. She pointed west, but not specifically, and said, "That way." She asked us to sit and gave us cookies and tea. We thanked her for her kindness and left in the direction she had indicated,, climbing down to the valley. The path was very sloppy, leading us between walls which held narrow strips of dirt in which some crop was planted. Half the distance down to the valley we spotted a couple working on one of those strips. The man, who had only one arm, struggled to help his wife. Franc approached the man and courteously asked him where the French border was. After a little pause, the farmer surprised us, "If you give us something out of your luggage I will provide you with the information. We put our heads together to decide what to give them. That was the only time they asked me to help in the decision since they needed to include one piece of my clothing for the couple. Luckily we had some clothes which we had received from the Red Cross in Cremona, so we gave them one dress and one pair of pants from that lot.

We feared the man wouldn't keep his promise, but he did. "The French border is on top of those Alps," he said, "but be careful in the valley by the creek. It could be dangerous." Well, now we knew where we needed to go, but when we looked up there, cold sweat ran down our faces. We walked down the hill, reaching a spot where a small church sat, making that enchanting place even more distinctive. From the church, we could see the creek we had been warned about. The man had informed us of dangerous predators who could check us for papers. Maybe he had exaggerated the situation a little, but it made our decision more complicated. Ivan surprised me by volunteering to be first to go down by the creek. "I will check it out and then come back to get you three," he said.

We thought he would return soon, but we waited and waited. He never came back. What could we think but the worst? There was nothing to do but go down and look for Ivan, even if someone was holding him. The creek wasn't far away. We could see down there, but we didn't see Ivan. When we got closer, I looked across the creek. There was Ivan, waving to us from under a fig tree! He signaled us to come. We couldn't believe that he had done that and scared us so badly. He had been worried constantly about being taken back to jail; he had wanted to be certain he was not returned to the communists, but nobody else was at that creek. He was running from a danger that did not exist. When we calmed down, we sat under the tree and ate the ripe figs, the only food we had eaten since the cookies that morning.

We rested a little, discussing where to turn for then on. We decided to take a path which extended about 500 feet into the mountain. We passed by a woman watching her cattle munch succulent grass. We could walk comfortably for awhile until we came to a point at which we had no choice but to climb up that rocky mountain. At least we did find a path by one giant rock which had frightened me as I looked at it from below. Had we been tourists, we could have appreciated that beautiful hill studded with gorgeous homes and the towering Alps topped with September snow. To our west was a valley containing a small church and a creek from which clear water emptied into the ocean. We were, of course, definitely not tourists, and had no time to enjoy the heavenly scenery. Therefore, we left that area. . . and, in my opinion, entered hell.

Up and up, we continued our climb on a narrow path, following wherever it led us. After a long struggle we were not only surprised but shocked to find an older man actually living there with several of his sheep. No matter which way we looked, we could see nothing but rocks on almost half of that peak. There was a space

164

about 100'x100', not completely clear of rocks, where he had only a narrow strip of land between the rocky walls, on which to tend his vegetables. The shepherd had built a cabin out of the rocks which surrounded him. We had expected to see snakes and lizards up there (snakes we didn't see, but lizards we did), but not living people. We asked him for the way up the mountain, and he pointed northwest to a path leading up. I wondered why he wasn't living down in the green valley. Most likely he didn't want to live with other people close; he found company just with his sheep and rocks. People must be born with the kind of personality to live without other people around them. Even though we often have disagreements, most of us need one another.

At each stage of our climb we took some rest to recover a little energy. We didn't have much time to waste; the hours were going by fast, and we were still not even half way to the top. When we did arrive about half way up the mountain we were surprised again. We came upon one or two other families who really lived up there in that wilderness of rocks. I wondered are these people in their right minds, or are we who left a place where the earth was green and the soil was workable? The families lived in some kind of shed. They had a concrete tank in which they captured water that was green and dirty. By then we were nearly dying of thirst, so we asked if they had any drinking water. No, they replied, but we were welcome to drink from that tank, which I declined to do. Even after all these years, I still wonder what they were doing up there. If they had to bring food and water from the valley by donkey, those things would be gold to them, and no one can blame them for not sharing.

By that time we were thirsty, hungry and exhausted from that climbing carrying all of our possessions. The men were near collapse from carrying our luggage, so I took one up the cliff through which we had to pass. That was probably the last hurdle for us then. When we cleared it, we came to a somewhat better surface near the top; we began to see fewer giant rocks, more ground and even some grass. Suddenly we heard somebody walking down toward us, and we ran behind some of the bushes up there. Who knew who that man was? He could be a guard on the Italian side of the border or he could be merely a man who had wanted to visit the top of the mountain. When the coast was clear, we neared the summit, and heard a gift from heaven – the sound of clear, delicious water bubbling up from under some small rocks. After we drank and rested for a short time, we hurried to meet our biggest hurdle, the French border.

Franc volunteered to go ahead to scout the area. He walked up there to a small cabin which was, as we thought, on the border. He signaled that it was safe for us to come to him, and we rushed to where he was. Although we hadn't eaten for forty-eight hours by that time, I felt healthy and strong. All of us looked all right under the circumstances. There was no marker indicating the Italian-French border, but the cabin gave us the impression that this was it. We were relieved to at least be on French soil, even if we were quite a way from any city. What adventures the last two days had given us! We felt lucky that there was still some daylight left as we stood on top of that mountain.

At last we had come to the point where we were able to slide down instead of climbing up, so from there we slid down to a place of level ground, where we found an empty cabin. Looking around, we saw where some of our people on the same journey as we were had signed their names. We rested for a short time, trying to determine how to get down to the city we could see below, but there were only cliffs on that side. We decided to turn south on a path, but a little farther out we met a hunter carrying his gun on his shoulder. There was nothing else to do but to ask him for directions down to a city. He said to follow him, so we did. We approached a building and he pointed to a road down from that building and said "That road will take you to Menton." He went into the building, and we followed the road, winding down and down for six kilometers. By that time it was completely dark; at least we knew where we were going, and that was down instead of up.

In Menton, a coastal city, we spotted a bus stop and close to midnight we were on a bus headed to Nice. We found a hotel there where we could stay after our long, arduous voyage. It was wonderful to lie down in a bed and finally get some rest. When we woke up, we wished we could stay longer, but we had to move out to avoid paying for another day. Because we hadn't eaten for sixty hours, we first looked for a restaurant and found one which had chairs and tables out on a terrace. After we had eaten, Ivan and Franc again took charge, telling me and the old man to stay there while they went to the railroad station to find out when the train would go to Paris. They came back, announcing that the train would go at 6:00 p.m. that same day.

They left us sitting there with our luggage again while they went to see the ocean and walk through the city. Franc's father and I were lucky that the restaurant manager didn't ask us to leave since we didn't order anything else all day . . . or worse, he might have called the police, and Ivan and Franc would not know where we had gone. But fortunately, we were able to sit there all day without being able to speak French or Italian, until Ivan and Franc returned. Finally they did, but said they did not have enough money for all four of us to go to Paris. I couldn't help but remember how Ivan and Franc had wasted money drinking every evening in Italy, but it was too late to change their habits. I did have enough dollars for Ivan and me, but Franc and his father didn't have any left. The only advantage to traveling with them was that Franc spoke Italian. Franc even said, "Let's leave my father here and go without him."

We didn't want that to happen, and replied, "No matter what we do, all four of us will do it together."

We decided to buy tickets to a place two stops before Paris. We did have enough money for that. We traveled all night long in one car by ourselves. Whenever an agent came to see our tickets, we pretended to be sleeping. At dawn, we noticed high-power lines leading to the city and thought that Paris must be near. We knew for sure when that same man came to our car and told us we were close to Paris; therefore, he had to see our tickets. Checking them he said, "You passed the stop your tickets were for." Franc tried to talk to him in Italian, which he didn't understand. We all did understand when he asked us if we had money to pay our way into Paris. Ivan took out the little he had. This paid Ivan's ticket, but there was no more money for the rest of us. The agent left us on the train and went to notify the police as we pulled into the Paris station.

The police took us to City Hall, where they handed us over to someone who processed our papers. Obviously, the authorities were used to handling people from Eastern Europe. We thought we would get treated kindly as we had been by the Italian police when we crossed from Yugoslavia. It was not the same, and we were to experience real French law a bit later in the day, and it would shock us. We expected them to take us to the Red Cross when they finished with our papers, but they did not. As we waited, we met two Croatian men who had come from the Red Cross. We were happy to see anyone who could help us, or at least advise us. They said they had to go to the Red Cross for dinner or they wouldn't get to eat that evening. We sat in that office all day long waiting and talking with a young Russian immigrant who had arrived in Paris four months ago. Our Slavic languages were similar enough that we could understand each other.

We were finished before the Russian, so we went out on the street to decide how to get to the Red Cross. Our friend Miha Trzok had sent us an address he had gotten from the Italian Red Cross. I remember seeing a flower stand (which I later would recognize in a movie) just outside City Hall. There wasn't time for the luxury of appreciating Parisian beauty, but it stuck in my mind because that was the first thing I saw when we left the police station as free people. We had papers now, but we wished the police had provided some kind of shelter for us. They didn't care that we had come to work in their country. They had given us only a document to show if anyone checked us.

On the corner we noticed a sign for the Metro entrance. The subway could take us where we needed to go, but we didn't know how the system operated and we didn't have any money for tickets. We got in the entrance and just looked at each other – what now? After a few minutes, that young Russian man we had been talking to nearly all day approached us, asking where we were going. Franc explained our predicament. The Russian, not given to small talk, simply took the paper with the address on it and told us to follow him. At the ticket window, he bought five tickets. We entered a train but the Russian still didn't talk much. Since Ivan was suspicious of anyone who was a stranger, he said to me, "He could be a Russian agent looking for people like us who have left communist countries." Nothing like that had ever entered my mind, but Ivan never trusted anyone.

When we got to one stop, the Russian got off the train, motioning for us to follow him down a long hallway and up steps till we got above ground. The Russian knew where he was going because he had been there when he first came to Paris, although he didn't tell us that, so Ivan reluctantly followed him, last, of course. We were pleasantly surprised to see Miha Trzok, the friend who had been with Ivan and me on that trip from Croatia.

This was now September 19, and we had left with Miha three months before, on June 20. By that time it was dark, but Paris streets had plenty of lighting. We parted from our Russian friend with our thanks for his help, but we didn't think to ask him his name and address.

We never forgot his kindness. Ivan and I would always talk about him when we remembered Paris. We would remember others, too, who helped us when we had nothing. In the years we traveled through Europe, many people were good to us and we to them. None of us had money, family or security. We all were poor, and all of us needed help. We had no idea what awaited us or where we would end up, but we knew we would work to make money for our future, no matter where that would be.

Now, three months after we had left home, we were starving, desperate to get a job for food, clothing, and most important, a room of our own. It did not have to be big, just big enough for the two us to sleep in a dry place and eat my own cooking. We were not even at that modest point yet and needed only a dry place to stay. Miha took us to the Red Cross, but they refused to take us in that first night. Miha had no money to lend us for a hotel. He could give us only enough to buy some bread. He and others who were already sleeping and eating in the Red Cross shelter advised us to do what they had done when they first came to Paris – sleep in a close, small park by a little canal. For four days and three nights we slept half the night in Nice, but it was already chilly at night in the park, so we often went across the street to walk and sit to keep warm. We went again to the Red Cross, who took me because I was a female, but they refused to take the men for another three days. However, some Croatian students in Paris had come to the Red Cross looking for someone to share their apartment. They took Ivan, Franc and Franc's father for those three nights, proving again the kindness of our people. After three days, the four of us were reunited at the Red Cross with a dry place to sleep and meals twice a day.

The strain of dealing with our desperate situation began to get to me, and later in the week I lay in bed with a high fever. Red Cross people told me I shouldn't be in bed during the day, but I explained how sick I was. If I was that sick, they said, I had to be in the hospital, so that was where I ended up. There I found two other Croatian ladies; one of them was Ana Rehoric, from Ribnik County. With her husband Janko and little daughter Katy, she had been in Goricia and Cremona with us. Since none of us spoke French, It was a little bit nicer for us to be together. Later on, an old lady came from her bed, asking where we were from. When we said, "We came from Yugoslavia," she began talking to us in a language which we could understand. She had come to France from Macedonia thirty years ago and had never spoken that language since. She was interested in prices in Yugoslavia for eggs, chickens and other goods. She told us, "I was sick when I came to this hospital, but hearing my language for the first time in all these years has made me well enough to go home." Poor woman, we never found out how she had come to France without any contact with her own people. Perhaps she had been stolen from her own country.

Chapter 10: **A Change in Lifestyle**

When my fever was down, I left the hospital and returned to the Red Cross center. It was better than sleeping in the park and having nothing to eat. It was warm, and we slept in small single beds, husbands and wives separately. We were kept busy going from one institution to another to get papers allowing us to work. We got our first document September 19th, and a few other documents followed one by one. One was a refugee card followed by a residential card and then a social security and work permit card. Finally we were able to go to the unemployment office. Here we received addresses of businesses offering work and another where we could pick up some clothes which were free of charge. They asked whether I preferred to work at the same place as Ivan's or to work at another place where the job would be easier. I chose to work with Ivan, so they got us work at a Citroen car factory, located by the Garibaldi Metro. Getting a job in Paris at that time was no problem, but getting an apartment in the city was another story.

The French authorities had provided us with jobs, but they didn't care where we would live. We people from Yugoslavia always helped each other; we turned to them for advice on getting a place to stay, no matter what kind it was. Our people already lived all over Paris, so they gave us the address of an older hotel where we got a room, although no ironing or cooking was allowed. I had bought an iron in Italy and had carried it across the mountains, but it didn't work in France, and I wouldn't be allowed to use it if it did. After a time, the hotel gave us a room where we could cook and we bought a little kerosene stove to cook on. We also bought another iron which we warmed on the stove. We used these things for the three and a half years that we were in Paris.

We had gotten our work permits in three weeks, and we began our jobs after living in the Red Cross for 21 days, nearly their one-month limit. The Red Cross had paid our rent for the first week at the hotel because we had left the shelter early.

Since we didn't know the right route to get to the factory, we were late for work on our first day at Citroen, but others told us the right way to get there, so we never were late again. An older man who spoke Czechoslovakian helped translate for us. We could understand each other because our Slav language is similar. The Citroen company asked if we needed an advance on our salaries, which, of course, we did. They gave us a week's wages, a generosity that surprised me. With the money from the Red Cross and from Citroen, I was able to buy a light coat, a sweater and a skirt. These were really needed for the chilly October weather. I had never worked in any factory, especially in a car factory with all those machines producing parts. To Ivan it was nothing unusual; he had worked in a Karlovac factory before we were married. I will never forget the first wages I got, the very first time I had received money for my work.

When I first came to work, my boss looked me over and asked if I was strong enough to work with the men. Some other women also worked there. Sometimes it was hard and sometimes not, but our normal six-day work week was more than plenty for me. Because we had no refrigerator, I also had to shop every day at the supermarket and then cook the meal. Ivan didn't work in the same department, but we were able to eat together and travel to work and back together. When we lived at the place named La Fourche, we often would walk to work and back.

It had been four months since we left our home, but finally we had come to the point where we could live on our own money instead of charity from the camps and the Red Cross. We had started working on October 10, 1957. Since that day, we were never again without money for the most important things we needed.

Of course, I couldn't say that everything was fine while we lived in that one room, without refrigeration or a normal stove. To eat in a restaurant would have been too expensive, and we needed to save for future security. It would have helped if I could have bought our fresh food on the way home from work, but often store owners closed their places at mid-day, reopening them at 4:00 p.m.; when we worked the day shift we worked from 6:00 a.m. to 2:30 p.m. and were home before the stores reopened. I washed our clothing by hand, a few pieces at a time so I could dry them on a window, the bed, the table, or the two chairs in our room.

After we came to America, people said, "La-la-la. You lived in glamorous Paris? What was it like?" It would have been wrong to say it wasn't exciting at all. We had come from a hard farm life and didn't stay inside much anyway. The Paris streets offered so much to be seen – people walking everywhere, going to movies, parks or coffee shops. In the evenings, streets were packed with people and lights glittered on buildings; during the day, tourists clicked their cameras to capture the historical architecture.

(Ivan in the park , , , with pigeons.)

On Sundays, Ivan and I would walk all over the city to see those famous places that tourists

visit. The summers there were mild, so sometimes we walked all day, although by afternoon my feet hurt from the high heels that all ladies wore then. We had to be dressed nicely all the time; even at work we wore nylon stockings every day to fit in with the crowd and never stepped out on the streets dressed casually. The men usually had on suits. The women wore long skirts or dresses, about ten inches under the knee, no slacks. Clothes were expensive there, so we had only a few nice outfits to wear wherever we were going.

(I pose above at the church Sacre-Coeur.)

I knew how to make my own clothes, but I didn't have a sewing machine. I did make one dress by hand. It was in the new style, short to the knee and narrow without a cut in the waist. I made my dress that way because I like to be different; soon after, the style in Paris changed from longer to shorter, the same as the one I had made.

When we had first started to work at Citroen, we each were given an outfit to wear on the job. Mine was at least two sizes too big for me. I wasn't comfortable wearing something I didn't look good in, and Ivan wanted me to look nicer, too, so when we could afford to purchase something better, we went shopping. We found cotton blue pants and a yellow top which fit me nicely. Approached my machine the next day, my boss glanced at my new outfit, saying, "Oh, madam Jarmek, you look nice today."

After I changed my outfit, one Croatian lady at work began picking on me, even though she had never spoken to me before. When I went to lunch, she put grease on my push button machine so that when I started to work I would get grease on my hands. Some French ladies told me who had done this, so I ran after her but couldn't catch her. One more time she got me, but that was the last time. She came to my station, telling me that our boss had asked me to come to his desk. When I came to him and said, "Did you ask for me to come here," he said, "No, I didn't." I looked at the woman, so did he, and then I went to confront her. She had already disappeared, and said later, "Oh, it's April Fools Day," to which I replied, "Maybe it is April Fool to you to do mean things to people, but to me that is never April Fool." I never spoke nicely with her again, except what I had to at work.

It was a joy for Ivan and me to absorb much of the city's splendor. We visited many of the parks in Paris, as well as some of its elegant museums and, of course, the Eiffel Tower. Walking by the River Seine was always enjoyable, many of its bridges offering gorgeous statues for us to admire. There were also three zoos which we visited from time to time when we had enough of the central city. Because zoos were located on the edge of the city, they were surrounded by plenty of green trees, grass and flowers, which pleased me. Paris is so large that it is impossible to see all of it in days or even weeks, but we were there long enough to appreciate most of it.

When I was ten years old, my parents had described France and other countries which were engaged in the war, so I had known a little about France before we lived there. One of our neighbors, Ivan Bosiljevac, my childhood friend Drago's father, had been in France during the war. Many times he had visited my father just to chat and tell him about his experiences there.

Many people did live a beautiful life in Paris -- spacious apartments in the city where they worked and houses in the suburbs where they enjoyed weekends. Many made a good living with their small shops, thousands of which dotted the streets of Paris. Those who were born in Paris had few problems finding apartments, but those who just gotten there had problems whether they had come from another country or from another place in France. It was easier for us to tolerate our conditions when we saw most French people living the same way we did. We had good jobs with good wages and could have afforded a better place to live. As a matter of fact, we paid more for that one room in an older hotel than some people did for an apartment. Too bad that we couldn't get one unless we bought it, and we weren't ready to make that decision unless we gave up our dream of America and stayed in Paris.

The French system was good for some things but not for others. It was good for its government health insurance and the law and order it kept to protect its people. But there was a strong element of control for all residents: When we found a place to live we had to visit the closest regional office to register where we were staying. They gave us papers to show police if they checked on us. If we had moved to another place we would have had to inform them. This rule was not just for those from other countries, but for everyone living in the city.

The system was not designed to protect tenants from landlords' abuses. When we lived in that hotel, it was the law that the rent must be lowered after a few months, but the landlords had their tricks: By arrangement with another landlord, each would send his tenants for one day to the other's hotel. If the tenants could be trusted, they would not use that trick. They sent Ivan and me only once in the beginning. The law was the same for apartments. The law stated, "Through many years of paying rent, the family almost pays for that apartment in full." From that point on, the rent would be small, which is why people didn't move from one place to another.

Everybody makes some mistakes during a lifetime, and so did Ivan and I when we searched for a larger place with smaller rent. Being young and not well informed, we didn't consider things like heating and the distance from our work. Ivan worked with an older Croatian who had lived in Paris for many years, was married to a French woman who had three grown children. One day he asked Ivan, "How would you like to live in a house with two large furnished rooms?" He went on to describe how his stepdaughter was going to Africa with her three children. Her husband was in the army there, and she and the children would stay there for two years. Before she left, she would like to find someone to rent the house, which was outside the city, while they were away. As her stepfather John knew Ivan well, he recommended us as a couple who could be trusted in the family's home.

Ivan and I went to see the place during the summer and fell in love with it. It was a gated property where a French family lived in the beautiful, large house. An unfinished house was being built by a Croatian man and his wife who lived in Paris. This was a dream house, something like one in a story book. It was small and cute with a nice garden and flowers. Surrounding this house were others belonging to people who worked in Paris but came there on weekends to enjoy the fresh air and greenery – which were inadequate for those of us in Paris. Not far away was a forest which we could see from the yard.

In the one room where we were living, we would come home from work exhausted, and Ivan usually lay down to rest while I bought food and cooked. Our neighbor lady, a Croatian named Angela, had nothing to do or anybody to cook for; therefore, she really got on our nerves when, with cigarette in her hand, she popped in as soon as we came home. Her husband worked at night, and their two children were staying far away in the countryside. Angela got bored being alone in her small room, so she visited us -- too often. She wasn't my kind of person; her conversation didn't fit my interests. But we didn't wish to be unkind to her, so we decided we would rather take this opportunity to move than to tell her not to come over any more.

Our new place was a paradise compared to the one we had just left. It was in a suburb on the north side of Paris, not far from the river Seine, which also ran through Paris. It was a quiet neighborhood, almost too quiet since we were now used to the activity in Paris. Not too far away was a small city center where we could do some shopping and go to the movies. We had two large rooms, uncarpeted but furnished. There was no central heat, something we didn't even think about that summer. The stove burned either wood or coal. There was a second floor where the lady had stored things she asked us not to use.

We had gotten away from the roaring boulevards of Paris and some tedious people there, but we had also gotten away from some good friends we had made there. We knew Franc and his father missed us, although we wouldn't say we missed them too much. We found out that there was no transportation there that would enable us to arrive at work on time, so we needed to buy some kind of vehicle. Ivan didn't mind buying a motorcycle, but I hated spending money we were saving for future needs. I think we all have to go through many mistakes before we learn how to make wise decisions. So we paid $400 for a new Pulman motorcycle.

John and his wife came to visit us almost every Sunday. Ivan and I had learned a little French, but fortunately, John spoke good Croatian and often acted as translator. We had lunch together as they had done when their daughter was there in the house we rented. As she was a good cook, John's wife usually brought food for all of us. She prepared her dishes in the French way and taught me how to eat French style. To show us how dinner is served, she sometimes brought an aperitif *(a drink tasting like licorice which turns white when mixed with water, drunk before dinner to whet one's appetite).* Then dinner is served with a bit of cheese or any kind of fruit as a dessert. She would bring oranges, apples, pears or bananas. When she brought bananas for the first time, Ivan said, "I once was very sick when I ate bananas. It would be best for me not to eat any." But she replied, "It will not hurt you. Nobody gets sick from them." Ivan should have refused, and I was frightened because he didn't want to disappoint our friend who called me her new daughter. Sure enough, when they left that afternoon, Ivan began repeating his unbelievable ordeal because he had eaten bananas. We got on our motorcycle and drove to the pharmacy, asking them if they could give him something for his pain, but they gave us nothing so we returned home to wait till the pain should stop. We had nobody there, no telephone or friends to whom we could turn for help. We learned then another mistake we had made going far from the city where we could have gotten help. After throwing up for an afternoon and evening, Ivan's stomach had calmed down. When John and his wife came the following Sunday, we told them, "No more bananas for Ivan!" After that experience, Ivan never ate bananas again. *(Many years later he smelled a suspicious pudding served to him in a hospital and asked me to test it. When I tasted it, I knew he was lucky. It was indeed banana pudding.)*

We communicated very rarely with our friends in Paris because none of us had a telephone. This was not unusual in Europe for people who weren't wealthy or those who didn't have a permanent home as we did. Telephones, showers and central heating are in almost everyone's homes in the United States, but in Europe then, and even now in the 21st century, people frequently live without those conveniences.

Ivan and I had mixed feelings about Franc and his father. On one occasion Ivan said to me, "You know it hurts me that Franc and his father don't remember what we did for them, especially you, who washed and ironed their clothes as long as we were together. Also, we paid the fare for their trip from Nice to Paris, and they never mention it. If Franc were a little considerate, he would buy some little thing to give you in thanks for all you did for him." I was touched that Ivan was concerned for me, perhaps because he had always pushed me to do some service for others. Still, we had some kind feelings for Franc who went through such difficulties with us, and basically, he was a nice person in other ways.

Our beautiful summer was gone, and a frigid fall arrived very fast, followed by an even colder winter. Although the temperature rarely fell below freezing in Paris, riding a motorcycle wasn't fun without proper clothing. The house we lived in had been lovely during summer, but winter was another story. The house was built of solid stone with a cement floor. Neither the kitchen nor the bedroom was carpeted. When we worked the first shift we were able to make a fire in the stove, but working evenings and coming home after midnight, we simply climbed into our cold bed and covered ourselves enough to sleep. We remembered our warm room in the Paris hotel with nostalgia. It began to look as though I had caught a cold, but this sickness didn't go away, even after a week or two. I was in pain all over – my teeth, head, back and chest all hurt. I began visiting doctors and dentists, but none could really figure out what was wrong.

In February, 1959, we moved back to Paris, a few blocks from La Fourche where we had lived previously. Our closest Metro was Guy Moquet on St. Ouen Boulevard, near the edge of the city's center. We often walked to work in warm weather. We lived in a triangle formed by St. Ouen and another street. Our address was 7 Passage Legendre, Paris 17. (The building number, I noticed, was the same as that of the house in which I was born.) From the second floor window facing the street I could see St. Ouen Boulevard and hear the roars of those European cars which made quite a noise from 5:00 a.m. to late at night. We had moved there to give me a warm place to rest, but it wasn't enough. I also needed a quiet place to sleep at night and a place to cook our meals – neither of which we now had. I asked our landlady to give us another place where I could cook and rest, especially when we worked the night shift and needed to sleep during the day. After two months of exhaustion, we got a room on the third floor with a small kitchen containing a two-burner gas stove. This was my haven. Our window now faced a courtyard, which gave me an opportunity to dry clothes, but I missed seeing what was going on out on the street.

Ivan and I made $100 each, $200 total monthly income, while working at Citroen. For this new room our rent was $36/month. The house in the suburb had been only $28/month. I tried to budget our daily meals at two dollars a day, but some days more because Ivan and I had agreed we would never be hungry again as long as we had money in our pockets. We no longer needed the motorcycle, so after a while we sent it to my brothers in Croatia.

Sometimes we met with our friends, but we still didn't look for Franc, who enjoyed spending his money on good times. Miha Trzok left for Canada while we were living out of Paris, but we had seen him before he left. Ivan and Miha were more like brothers than friends, both honest and kind. Miha was a special friend also because the three of us had left Croatia together that day, June 20, 1957; we had jumped the border fence together on June 22 in the city of Goricia as we began our hard road to America. It looked as if Miha's way was to Canada. It was easier to immigrate to Canada than to America, so Miha got his papers in 1958, long before we got ours to America.

At our new place, we found out that a Croatian couple named Zvanko and Ana lived only one-half block away. They came from Ozalj County, not far from Ribnik County. We began to socialize with them, playing cards and walking together on Paris streets. We got along well together, but as was often the case whenever we met nice people, they soon immigrated to Canada. Ana's sister Ljubica worked with me at Citroen, but she had gone to Canada before Ana. Another couple, Stanko and Ana, from Dalmacia, Croatia, became good friends also, but shortly they got their papers for Canada.

We were able to make some of these friends through the church. Our priest once organized a bus trip to a gorgeous place outside of Paris. It was on the same side of the city as Orly Airport, which we passed on our way. We arrived at a forest area where there was a small chapel and a hall with kitchen and dining areas. After we enjoyed the food they had prepared for us, we strolled through the forest with our priest, looking down on a little river as it murmured slowly below us. Somebody with a camera took pictures of those of us there, so we posed with a husband and wife, Stanly and Ana. I still have the snapshot, but our acquaintance with them was destined to be short. Once we attended a movie together, but soon after that they too left for Canada.

(Ivan and I admire the roses with Ana and Stanly.)

(Below, from left to right: Josip and Milka Krznaric, I and my husband Ivan in Paris. Josip and Milka immigrated to Kansas City one year later than we did.)

Chapter 11: **All that Glitters Isn't Paris**

We continued living at Passage Legendre where everything was convenient, and we were able to walk to work often when the weather was pleasant. However, my health wasn't good, and the stone house where we had lived in the country had contributed to my illness. It was nothing serious but enough to prevent my doing the hard manual labor I had been doing. My stomach was upset if I ate anything before I went to work, so I would do that heavy work on an empty stomach. My doctor didn't bother to give me anything for my acid condition, and I hadn't heard of any medicine other than aspirin. In Croatia we hadn't even had that. At home, the treatment for a common cold, for example, was curd with linden tea, which was very simple to get from our fragrant linden trees.

I had gone to both of the Yugoslavian doctors in Paris because they spoke our language, but now I began to search for a French doctor. My French was not fluent, but good enough to tell him how I felt. From a sign on the other side of St. Ouen, I got the name of a doctor within walking distance. At that time appointments weren't necessary, so I just walked in. An older doctor asked what I needed. After I explained my problem, he took an x-ray of my upper body, and explained, "Your body is very weak. I can help if you are willing to come here twelve times for shots, one every other day." He also gave me some expensive pills for my headaches. After twenty-four days, he asked if I felt better, and I assured him, "I am a new person – no more headache, no more backache, and I feel much stronger."

That doctor had certainly helped that problem, but I still needed to find a good dentist. Several dentists had tried to treat the periodic severe pain in my upper left gums, even pulling some teeth *(which, I would discover seventeen years later, were not what caused my pain).* I believed I would just have to live with this condition for the rest of my life. It was only after developing sinus problems also that an American doctor took x-rays and discovered that although nothing was wrong with the sinuses, There was a cyst or polyp wedged between bones in a cavity. He told me that an operation could cure that pain. I had never been so happy to have a doctor say something was wrong with me! "Operate on me as soon as possible," I said, "I have to know if that is the reason for my long suffering." He operated the following week from inside my mouth, cutting through some facial bone. He got to that cyst, which was full of trapped fluid. After surgery my face and nose were swollen and painful, but it was over soon, and I never again had that awful pain in my gums.

Ivan and I had liked living in that nice small country house outside Paris, and we had enjoyed the nature that surrounded us there, but winter had brought us much trouble and had ruined my health, causing me to suffer for many years. Unlike me, Ivan was never sick during that difficult winter. Perhaps his system was stronger than mine.

After two and one-half years of working at Citroen, I decided to look for an easier job, even if I would be working without Ivan and would probably no longer have the same schedule. I found a job in a munitions factory, making bullets. The managers gave me work in a department where hunting shells were made from paper. My work was in control, to check if all printing was correct or if any shells were damaged. At first we did that manually, but two months before I left, the company bought two machines which could do the work much faster. Because of this, some ladies lost their jobs, but I was fortunate. A Slovenian lady and I were put on the new machines. All we had to do was look at the shells rolling by on the conveyor belt, but it did require sharp eyesight, which was why they gave the two of us that job. We worked nine hours a day, five days a week. That was regular time, no overtime. I made less money than I had at Citroen, but at least I was home on Saturdays to work and rest a little bit, which I really needed.

On my first day at my new work, I arrived for lunch in the cafeteria. One man was quite surprised to see me after a long separation from Ivan and me. It was Franc Cokel, our friend in Italy and our companion during the difficult trip to France. I wasn't completely surprised because Ivan had told me, "You probably will find Franc and his father at the Gevelot factory. Their first job was there, so they perhaps still work at the same place." Franc and his father were happy to see me after such a long time; on the other hand, I wasn't very enthusiastic about renewing our friendship. They never mentioned any of my help to them or appreciation for what we had done for them, especially the time we paid for their trip from Nice to Paris. Deciding not to hold a grudge forever, I pretended to be happy to see them. The following day I took a picture of Ivan and me to show them. As Franc was a sensitive person, his eyes became wet when we looked at Ivan's picture, and he asked me to arrange a get-together, so I invited them to our place the following Sunday.

I continued to eat with Franc and his father in the cafeteria, even though I didn't care for their conversation most of the time. I told Franc that we expected to get our clearance papers soon for entering the United States. That didn't sit well with him, so he tried to tell me how America had fallen behind Russia in technology. This was to distract me from our positive American feelings and change our minds about entering that country. He should have known that wouldn't work; after all, the reason we left Yugoslavia was so we could immigrate to America.

Our chance to go to America was always on our minds, so we constantly looked for ways to save money. We definitely did not want to get in the same situation we were in when we struggled up that rock-strewn mountain from Italy to France and began life in Paris without any money whatsoever. As we were still young in 1960, we made the same mistake as before. One major way to save money for our future was to find a place with lower rent. Some friends left for Canada, so we grabbed the opportunity to get their room for much lower rent, even though it didn't have central heat. Now we were living at 16 Rue Des Montiboeufs, Paris 20, Metro Gambetta. We moved in during the summer, so heat wasn't a problem for some time. Hot weather wasn't a problem at all. I don't remember feeling excessive heat there during the days, and the nights, with our windows open, were really pleasant. We never had flies to bother us in Paris, either. Winter isn't harsh there although rooms still needed to be heated.

Two young Croatian men lived in that same housing development. Ivan and I had met them through mutual friends. Jacob Barun and his cousin Miho Barun had come to Paris from Livno, Bosnia. We got to know some of their friends also, a fine group of Bosnian Croatians who later dispersed to different parts of the world. I remember Nikola Saric and his friend Stjepan, whose last name I don't recall. They would travel with us on the same plane to America. Their friend Luka Vujic married a girl named Barbara from Duga Resa, close to Karlovac. She worked with me in Gevelot, and we became good friends. Barbara's friend Ana also married a man named Ivan, but I lost track of them. Since those days in Paris, the only one of these people we have seen again is Miho Barun. After we came to America, we contacted him in Chicago when we Croatians were having a dance to benefit Croatians in Kansas City. I invited a group of musicians, and one of them turned out to be Miho's son, so Miho and a friend came with their sons also. We sometimes kept in touch, and learned that Miho married a girl named Zdenka from his homeland in Bosnia.

All of that time in Paris we waited and waited for our papers to enter the U.S.A. We had applied through my grandmother Jagas's brother, Matt Brozenic, who was close to 80 years old and had lived alone since his wife Dorty had passed away a few years earlier. He had immigrated to Pittsburg, Pennsylvania, when he was a young man. He and Dorty never had children. Uncle Brozenic was anxious to get us to America to assist him in his old age. We were equally anxious to reach our final destination so that we could settle down to work and secure our future.

We received an interesting letter of instruction from Uncle Brozenic dated March 2, 1959:

> *"Dear children, the weather here is a bit better, but as for me, I don't feel well enough. For this reason, I would be happy to have you here as soon as possible, so you can help me a little. I am sending you, dear Ana, two cards from my bank where I have some money deposited, but you have to sign to get this money, according to my written arrangement if anything is left after my death. For this reason I would like to see you here, but you should return these cards after having signed them so they are to be deposited at the bank. You should sign beside the sign of the cross below my signature."*

He was repeating his words to be sure that I was going to do the right thing with those cards.

Approval for immigration to America was going too slowly. Uncle Brozenic needed us, and we needed him, and we needed America. Neither he nor we, however, could speed up the process or change American law. Matt Brozenic had the same kind personality as his sister, Magdalena Jagas. During his whole life he was sensitive and totally unselfish. Matt and his wife had helped Magdalena and her children when they needed it the most. My mother, who was his niece, received a few dollars at the time when I was small, but during the war she couldn't communicate with him. Right after the war he began helping again, bringing his twin sister to Pittsburg where she married and had her own family. I hoped that the same unselfish spirit had also come through the family to me.

I signed those two cards and sent them back to him, thinking little about it. If I did receive something I would be happy to have that help, but if I didn't, my husband and I would still do well on our own. I had never asked Uncle Matt for anything except for those papers to let us come to America. I was just anxious to help him when we got to America. Although he never indicated how much money was in that account, he had said, "If you come here after I die, you will have something to begin your life in America."

Fate did take that different turn. Uncle Matt died February 15, 1960, before we were able to get to America. I had never told anyone except my parents about those two cards from the bank, but my mother had also received two cards from another account. After Uncle Brozenic died, his wife's niece, Milke Jarnevic, wrote me:

"Dear Ana, Uncle Matt died. I am writing because I know he was making papers for you and Ivan to come to America. Another purpose for me to write you is, we found your name on one of his accounts but as you aren't here, you can't get that money without somebody to represent you. I could get that money for you, but you have to send me a notarized letter so I can get that money and send it to you."

As honest as I am, and at that age a little naïve, I might have done as she asked. My husband, however, was always suspicious of others, so he advised me not to do as she suggested.

He was right. It wasn't a good idea to trust her. I wrote her:

> **"Don't do anything with that money. I will authorize my Uncle Marko Bosiljevac (my father's brother), who lives in Kansas City. He will go and do what is needed. I also will ask Uncle Marko to make papers for us now that Uncle Matt has died."**

Uncle Marko did make the trip to Pittsburg to see how matters stood at the bank. He was surprised when he arrived and learned that the children of Uncle Matt's twin sister and niece of his wife Milka Jarnevic had filed to fight in court for the money in my name and in my mother's name. Right after this, I received about six pages of court documents in Paris. Uncle Matt had left his will and other documents with his attorney, but his sister's family engaged him to defend them in court. Uncle Marko and my cousin Ana Markovic, hired another attorney to defend me and mother. Well, getting a lawsuit heard in court takes a long time, so it just sat in the system while Ivan's life and mine were still in Paris. It was so frustrating that we almost decided to stay in Paris after all.

In 1958 I had received a letter from my parents that contained surprising news. On January 18, 1951, when I was fifteen years old, my father had gone to visit his sister Dragica in Zegreb, and he had done something else when he was there. Father knew that Uncle Marko from Kansas City would like to get me to America, and it would give my father great pleasure if at least one of his children could immigrate there, so on that date he also paid a visit to the American Consulate where he signed me up under quota. During that time anyone could just forget about the possibility of fast immigration. Who would have thought that day would come? It had . . .

but too late for Ivan and me because we were no longer in Yugoslavia. I asked the American Embassy in Paris if that would do any good for us there. They sent information about me to the American Embassy in Belgrade requesting that my papers be transferred to Paris where I was living with my husband. My parents had told me in their letter that if I had family of my own they could also immigrate to America with me. Unfortunately, all this didn't do us any good because when I hadn't responded immediately they had altered my quota to another number.

It disturbed me when I thought how we could be immigrating to America without any difficulty if we hadn't left our home for one more year. Still, I don't regret leaving as we did; we were young and full of energy, and we had great adventures. Although we had gone through great difficulties, I remember it now as a happy time for us. My only regret for those four years is that in America we could have been making more money to save in that time, and we would have had four years of additional pensions, as well. Also, of course, we could have started our family earlier than we did.

Chapter 12: **We Adapt**

What had we learned about Paris in the three and one-half years we lived there? There was a lot to see – beauty, glory, history and excitement – and Ivan and I saw all of that and more. We also learned how the French lived, how they behaved and what they think normal life in Paris should be.

Some had become rich and famous and enjoyed a high life style. Others lived the same kind of lives as we did. The old hotels like the ones we lived in were inhabited mostly by French people from outside of Paris but who weren't able to find decent apartments. Tenants shared the one bathroom on the floor. Some hotels provided only one bathroom for two or three floors, and the walks up or down weren't glamorous or pleasant for any of us.

Most of the time, the French tenants didn't see themselves as poor, and, I have to admit, neither did we. They did have the advantage of their country's language and education, but otherwise, they were in the same position as we were. French people who had jobs paying them enough income to eat, dress and save for vacation thought they had good lives. They loved their city, but they also loved to leave it during the summers. Some of the large factories would close one week apart so that traffic out of the city could be eased somewhat. Even small food stores on the same street would close one at a time so that people could still find food in other stores.

Traffic was unbelievable on main highways during the summers. A mass of people would take to the roads, not only in France, but throughout Western Europe. Even tens of miles from large cities, traffic would be bumper to bumper until vehicles finally began spreading in different directions.

This is how important vacations were to Parisians. They talked about their vacation months before they left, asking each other what their plans were for the next summer. They went away at least two or three weeks a year, some having accumulated up to five weeks of time to use. When we first worked at Citroen, everyone who had been employed there for at least a year had to take their vacations at the same time. The first year, Ivan and I had two weeks paid leave. It was hard when friends asked us where we were going and we said, "We aren't going any place." "Why not?" they exclaimed, "It's fun." They didn't realize that we had never been on vacation. For us, just coming to  Paris had seemed, in some ways, like a vacation -- although it did turn out to be a long one for us.

We who stayed in Paris over the summer found it to be an unusual experience.

(Left to Right: Josip Pozeg, Jure Kucenic, I and Ivan)

Although the streets looked oddly empty, the tourist locations were all jammed and lively. As we passed by, we could hear mostly foreign languages coming from them. So, we found no need to leave with all the new and interesting things right there. Many of the French had gone to the countryside, but we had come <u>from</u> the countryside, so it was the city that attracted us. We noticed that the foreigners (not Ivan and I, of course) were usually behaving more poorly than the French. Loudest were the Italians, Spanish, Portuguese and Yugoslavs. Some foreigners, like those, seemed to want to shout at the world, "Look at me! I am different." The French didn't show off at all to be noticed. They didn't seem to pay attention to whether they were being watched or not. I had little experience with public behavior before we lived in Paris, but I watched how the French behaved and loved it, so I adopted their style for my own as quickly as I could.

Mingling with the groups of tourists around Paris, Ivan and I tried to guess what language people were speaking. Occasionally we heard our own, but we merely listened without identifying ourselves to them. Sometimes we went to movies. Once Ivan lost his billfold in a theater, so the next day he ran to look for it. A cleaning lady helped him look in those two seats where we had sat, and luckily Ivan found it behind his seat. He was very happy, since he had thought he would never see it again. We found most French people to be honest, but they didn't believe in helping homeless people. They would say, "In Paris there is plenty of work if anybody wants it, so go get a job." On the Metro they usually read something or just sat quietly. They did not drink alcohol to extreme, but usually had a limit. Once as Ivan and I walked past a coffee shop, two men threw a very drunk man on the sidewalk. They were very upset with the drunk's unmannerly behavior. When the French want to insult someone they may say, "You trash," or if very upset they might call them, "You shit." With us, most French people were friendly, although others were cold. Perhaps some remembered bad experiences with foreigners.

French girls usually avoided foreign men, but sometimes couldn't resist because of a man with very good looks. One nice looking French girl named Denise worked with me at Cirtroen. We became friends quickly when she learned I was from Yugoslavia. She was nice and good looking, so I wondered why she hadn't found a young Frenchman, instead of the Yugoslav named Milan that she lived with. She asked me if my husband and I would like to meet him. I tried to avoid that invitation. I knew the relationship wouldn't be permanent because Yugoslavians in France were there temporarily; all of us had plans to relocate to other countries. I even doubted Milan was his real name.

My friend, however, wouldn't take "no" for an answer, so we arranged for them to come to our one-room apartment. The young man told us he was from Novisad, Serbia. We conversed in French, but if he wanted to tell us something he didn't want her to know, he spoke Srbo-Croatian. "She wanted to live with me, although I didn't want her to," he said. "Then she stayed outside my building and cried till I took her in." He continued, "I have no intention of marrying her. I left my girlfriend in Novisad. One of these days when I settle down, perhaps in Australia, I will bring my girlfriend to me and we will be married." I felt very uneasy being in their company under such circumstances, and I also felt sorry for this nice French girl who had let herself get into such a situation. She was so happy and excited, but I was just the opposite – sad and worried about what would happen to her when the relationship ended. Not long after that I left that job and didn't see her again, but some of my friends told me that as I had predicted, she almost destroyed herself. She began to smoke and put on more weight, no longer caring how she looked. She didn't talk to people from Yugoslavia because of that one person who had hurt her. I was sorry for her, but grateful that I didn't work there anymore.

There were other similar cases, but not all of them ended up as sadly as hers. One Croatian man, Ivan Perkovic, was also in France at the same time we were.

He fell in love with a French girl while he waited for his papers to enter America. His plan was to come to Kansas City where he had some friends, but he waited until his wife, that French girl, could get her papers so that they could immigrate together. Ivan and Clodette have lived here in Kansas City ever since they arrived, two nice people who are loved by people from all countries. I have heard it said that French people are cold, but here is my story about those I knew. Many were warm, friendly people.

Summers in Paris had allowed us to see a great deal of that beautiful city, but our winters weren't too cold, either. Snow rarely fell; when it did, it melted right away except on the north side where we had lived in that small house. Still, winters seemed long without the sun shining, and I waited anxiously to bask in it again.

(Ivan and I enjoy spring in a Paris park.)

Early in the spring we finally saw it and rushed to the park to get some of that sunshine. On a Sunday when we had more time to spend, we went to a great park, a forest in Boulogne where many Parisians were enjoying

199

the sun and nature for the same reason. Boulogne is beautiful. Sometimes when I see a movie made in Paris and see actors riding in old fashioned carriages through the park of Boulogne, I remember, "I was there many times, sitting on that soft, green grass and walking on those flat roads under tall trees reaching up to the Paris sky." I remember the small lake with ducks paddling in it which we admired from the grass where we were lying. Boulogne was on the west side of Paris, not too far from where I worked the second time, a place called Issy Les Moulineaux South-West Paris.

When we were able to get into the countryside, the land was mostly level and fertile. We saw plenty of it when we got out of Paris a few times. Once, when we lived out in the suburbs, we went riding our motorcycle to Versailles where we registered the county where we had lived.

These are nice memories of those days, but others are also with me -- those which made my life hard and painful. We were young, without the responsibilities of children, which was fortunate because of the conditions under which we frequently lived.

We were not alone in finding life difficult at times. It hurt me greatly to see homeless people on the Paris streets, lying on the Metro rails to use the warm air coming from below to keep them from the winter chill. Shortly after we arrived in Paris I almost cried when I realized that the French authorities who had given us shelter did not help their own homeless. Later I found out that most of these were alcoholics who didn't want help because they wouldn't give up their drinking. Once while shopping inside a small, crowded store, a lady left her baby in its stroller out by a glass window through which she could keep an eye on it. She panicked when she noticed the baby was gone. The police found the stroller with the baby safely in it about two blocks away. We learned that homeless people kept all of their property in strollers when they could find one. In this case, the homeless woman hadn't seen the baby at first; when she did notice, she left the stroller and the baby and disappeared. The French had little sympathy for beggars, because during that time anybody who was willing to work could get a job. Ivan and I gave beggars money anyway because even if they were physically well they probably had mental problems. I am softhearted toward people who live in misery and wished I could help more.

A few times while we lived in Paris there were strikes against the underground transportation system. These made a big mess on the city streets. On one occasion we were still living at the Red Cross. We worked the night shift then, walking far from our shelter to get to work. Luckily, factory personnel took us back to the Red Cross in their truck. Otherwise, we would have had a long walk back in the very early mornings.

Croatian people tried to help each other in Paris, and it was such a help to newcomers like us. When we began working we found out that many Algerian men lived in Paris without women from their country whom they could marry. They had escaped the war with the French and came as refugees. Instead of turning them away, the French took them into their country to work. French women, however, didn't care to marry them. They weren't bad looking men, but they were Muslims. French women preferred blacks to Algerians. There at Citroen, many Algerians worked, causing no trouble at the work place. In other places, however, they often bothered ladies on the street. They would follow women, trying to get their attention. It happened to me twice, frightening me somewhat, but fortunately it happened where I could have gotten help if needed. The first time I was on my way home from the doctor's office. It was a nice sunny day, so I stopped in a small park by the boulevard where others also sat on benches. The Algerian came and sat on the same bench. When he tried to talk to me, I got up and walked in the crowd, hoping he would go away. When he didn't, I said, "There is a policeman ahead. If you are still bothering me when I get there, I'm going to tell him." Finally that did it. Algerians were afraid of police, who were aware of their habits.

The second time I wasn't so lucky as to have a policeman near. I had gone to a general store on St. Ouen Avenue, two blocks away from where we lived. Returning home, I was practically alone on the street. Suddenly a short Algerian man came from nowhere, following me. I knew what he was doing. He walked closely, at the same speed as I; when I stopped to look in store windows, he also stopped. I certainly didn't want him to discover where I lived, so I had to get rid of him there. I had two choices: to run in the store and tell them of the man following me, or to try to scare him away by myself. I chose to take matters into my own hands first; if that didn't work I would run in the store. I raised the wooden clothes brush I had just bought and lifted it high in the air, telling him, "If you don't disappear right now, I'm going to hit your head so hard you will never forget it!" He almost fell on his behind, saying, "I didn't do anything." "I know very well why you are following me," I replied. My tactic worked. He disappeared immediately.

I had learned to defend myself growing up with two brothers. I felt I was their equal – not just a weak female. Standing up to that Algerian, I was reminded of a story which my mother often told us when she was in a happy mood. It went like this: *The little rabbit said, "I am going to kill myself because I have to be afraid of everybody, but nobody is afraid of me." Then the rabbit went to the pond to drown himself. When he arrived he saw some frogs that jumped in the water when they spotted him. Little Rabbit was surprised and stopped at the edge of the pond. A quiet smile came over his face as he thought, "I am not going to kill myself after all. There is somebody in this world who is afraid of me."* I was never an aggressive person, but I did learn, not only with my brothers, but also with boys in our neighborhood, how to take care of myself. Learning how to stand up to aggressive men helped me greatly through my life. Although I am not young anymore, I still can defend myself vigorously if necessary. Hard farm life, too, helped me become stronger and braver. Coming to Paris brought a big change in learning to face all kinds of people, something I hadn't grown up with. I had never before seen people of different religions or different color, but in Paris I learned to deal with a real "mixed bag" of humanity.

Through many experiences, some good and some bad, we passed 1957, 1958, and 1959 in Paris. We watched other Croatians who had parents or siblings in America or Canada disappear to that world of our dreams. Ivan and I felt our youth slipping away without being able to settle down in one place. We enjoyed walking the boulevards and parks of Paris, but we came back to a one-room apartment in which we couldn't even plan a family. I had grown up in Grice and now had seen a larger world of which we desperately wanted to be a part. By 1960 we had become very restless . . .

(This picture sometimes reminded Ivan and me to leave our youth in Europe. We wanted to come to America to work, have children, and grow old together in our adopted country.)

Chapter 13: **America: Here We Come!**

After three years and nine months since we had left Grice, we finally got our visas to enter America. In 1960 we got the first papers to be processed for immigration, and something heavy lifted from my shoulders. Ivan, who had a steady job in Paris now began to worry whether or not he could get a steady job in the United States. I felt more positive because I felt we would find family there who would help us look for jobs. One month before we left Paris, two of our friends, Tony Mrvunac and George Kucenic, were already in Kansas City. (Tony's sister, Milka Krznaric, and her husband Joe had to stay in France for another year until Tony got a job and prepared a place for them.)

According to our documents, we left Paris on March 21, 1961, taking the train to Brussels, Belgium. A porter on the train asked us where we were going. When we said, "We are going to America," he smiled, "Tell John F. Kennedy, the newly elected president, 'Hello' for me." We had been following the situation in America through a Croatian radio station so we had some idea of what was going on in America.

(This picture is from one of my documents in Paris.)

Our trip had been paid for by Uncle Marko Bosiljevac, so the immigration agent in New York asked if we wanted to go to Kansas City by plane or train. With really no idea how long that trip would be, Ivan chose to travel by train. We left for Chicago sometime after dark that night. It was an exhausting trip, but Ivan had wanted to see the country as we went and felt we might not have another opportunity to see it. Although sleepless, we did marvel at the rich agricultural land we passed. While Ivan and I waited in an eating area, two Croatian men overheard us talking and asked Ivan if he would like to remain in Chicago and work for them in their shop. Ivan thanked them and replied "I would like to have a job so fast in America, but our family is waiting for us in Kansas City." We had left Grice as a team and survived rough travels together. When we arrived in Kansas City's Union Station at 1:00 a.m. on March 24th, very tired and sleepy, we were at least, still a team working together. Uncle Marko and Aunt Mary had waited for us until that late hour, and took us to their home to sleep.

After a much needed night's rest, we repaid Uncle Marko the money which he had paid and waited for the airline to refund the money for the airfare we hadn't used. Aunt Mary was surprised that we repaid them so quickly, but we had saved some of our money in Paris to do that. While we rested the next day, we met Uncle Marko's family who had come to meet us. We had brought gifts for all of them, particularly a blue crystal vase for Ana Roper. She had asked me to bring a vase for her, and I had paid $40 for this one (at a time when I could buy a coat for $20). We couldn't bring crystal in our luggage for everyone, but I later regretted not being able to bring some for ourselves.

Ivan was now thirty, and I was twenty-five. Our dream of coming to America was really coming true at last

We soon discovered that many people from Ribnik County lived in Kansas City. (My grandfather, Tomo

Bosiljevac, had found the same thing when he immigrated 54 years earlier.) Uncle Marko and Aunt Mary asked their friends to help us find jobs quickly. Many of those Croatians already knew who we were. Unattractive jobs were readily available here in 1961, but good ones were more difficult to find. Five days after we arrived, Zlatko Frankovic, who had left Ribnik County about ten years earlier, found work for Ivan in the factory where he worked. The company polished marble monuments. Ivan's hourly pay was $1.50, and he brought home $52 a week, which we thought was good since in Paris he had made only $25 per week. I was kind of weak from hard work in Paris, so my aunt told me to rest before I started to work. Our relatives asked us to stay with them all summer until we could get acquainted, so I went to school to learn English, which would help me a great deal later on. Four months after we arrived, a lady named Charlotte Eatter (a Croatian lady born in Kansas City), found me a job in the dress factory where she worked. When I could not stay away from my mother's sewing machine at a young age, I had hoped that someday this skill could get me a job, and it did. I had to take a bus to get to work, and it was a long trip from the suburb where we were living. A job is a job, however – and I was used to doing things the hard way by then.

In the fall, my cousin Ana Markovic asked me to come to Pittsburg to see my attorney about my inheritance from Uncle Matt Brozenic. I hoped nobody on the train would ask any questions since I didn't speak English well yet, but quite the opposite occurred since those near me started a conversation first. I tried to explain that they wouldn't understand my English, but they said they could understand everything I said. That was when I fell in love with the American people who showed me their warmth and understanding. An African-American lady had traveled from Los Angeles to New York City to see her daughter. She and I talked all the way to Chicago, where she helped me get another train to Pittsburgh. A middle aged man sat next to me then, and started the questions again. When I said I had lived in Paris for over three years, he asked me quite a bit about it. Another lady on that half of the trip was also nice and friendly. At the station, I met cousin Ana and her husband, Ivan Markovic, for the first time in my life.

The next day, Ana and I visited the attorney's office where I signed a document that would pay him 25% of my inheritance if I ever got the money. Then I began calling some of my neighbors from Grice who now lived in Pittsburgh. My childhood friend, Drago Bosiljevac, came to see me with his new bride and his parents, Ana and Ivan Bosiljevac. Sofia (Bosiljevac) Jarnevic and her husband Ludva came too. Sofia, born in the same house (No. 5) as grandpa Tomo, was a daughter of grandpa's cousin Josip. I stayed to visit for a week before returning to my job making dresses.

When I returned to Kansas City, Ivan and I looked for an apartment of our own. Many Croatian families were living in Wyandotte County, so it was easy to find rentals owned by people whose families we had known in Ribnik. Charlotte, who had found a job for me, also found us a small furnished apartment with two large rooms, a bedroom and a kitchen which we also used for a living room. Our address was 634 Barnett Avenue, a spot where our new City Hall now sits. The owners of that house were Paul and Mary Secen. Mary was the lady who had talked with those American airmen who parachuted from their planes during WWII.

The only furniture we needed to buy was a television set. In February, 1962, we paid $245 for a black and white Philco. That cost many weeks worth of Ivan's wages. The following summer we didn't get much sleep because our apartment wasn't air-conditioned.

My job at the dress factory wasn't steady. Sometimes they sent me home when they were out of the kind of work I was doing, and other times they called me at midday to come in. The Secens' daughter-in-law was a nurse, so she asked me to work at Saint Margaret Hospital doing the same kind of sewing as at the dress factory. I started at $1 an hour, bringing home $35 every week. Ivan was contributing $62, and we were paying $50 a month, including utilities, for our apartment. Our groceries ran about $15-$20 per week, so my wages covered rent, utilities and groceries while Ivan's went in the bank for future needs.

We had been married for seven years, and had saved some money, so it was time to start our family, although we had no house or car, and only a single piece of furniture, the TV. I got pregnant near the end of 1962, but miscarried. In the spring of 1963 I got pregnant again, and we moved to a little larger, unfurnished apartment with three rooms and a shared bath. I was extremely sick during the first of my pregnancy and was not able to work. My boss at the hospital never understood, but I finally got some medicine from the doctor which helped.

For the first time we had our own furniture, but we still did not own a car. I still took the bus to work while Ivan rode with a coworker. We bought a portable washing machine which we set up in the basement two stories down. People in the old country thought everyone in America lived the good life. They didn't realize that immigrants had to work very hard and save money out of their small weekly paychecks in order to have an easier life in years to come. The summer of 1963 was very hot, so life wasn't easy for me with my first child, although it wasn't as hard as my mother's life had been.

Finally the hot summer was over. Although I had become very heavy with the pregnancy I continued to work at St. Margaret's. Just three days after my 28th birthday, I was cutting some sheets when an old lady named Tellie returned from her lunch hour. She was talking slowly as she said, "I passed by the waiting room where people are watching a sad story on TV. In Dallas, just now, President John F. Kennedy was shot." Like millions of others, we had admired him for his compassionate programs to help the poor and were shocked that he had been assassinated, not in a communist country, but here in America.

I worked for two more weeks because the doctor told me we could expect our baby at Christmas time. It didn't happen quite that soon, but it did come close to being a New Year's baby. On Sunday, December 29,  1963, the sky was full of snowflakes early in the morning. I turned to Ivan and exclaimed, "It looks like today is the day when our baby will be born." We still didn't have a car, but a young couple named Ed and Francis Secen lived on the first floor, and they offered to take me to Providence hospital. The doctor sent us back home, saying, "That baby will be born in one month, not today." We returned home and I put a chicken (which I forgot to salt) in to bake. We ate lunch, but Francis and I decided to return to the hospital where my labor pains came closer all afternoon. God's decision, not the doctor's, chose the time, for at 10:45 p.m. our baby girl was born. We named her Simone, a name we had chosen in France. *(Our daughter Simone above.)*

Our apartment was nice and warm through that winter, but summer was another story. We had some savings, but we needed too many things, and the most important one was a car. Ivan went once or twice to learn driving techniques, and he came home one day to tell me he had gotten his driving license. We bought a Pontiac with front bucket seats for $1,200. The original price one year earlier had been $2,200. When we bought it, it had only 4,000 miles on it, and we just took over the payments from the previous owner. (**First car below.**)

Ivan parked the new car in front of our apartment because nobody had a garage in that part of town. Imagine our shock when Francis ran upstairs the next day calling to Ivan that somebody had hit his car! We ran downstairs and saw two older people, one of whom was our apartment owner, Ana Horvat. The other was her sister's husband. Ana had been teaching him how to drive. The man was frightened, but assured us he had insurance so our car would be fixed. That man never drove a car again. We were, of course, upset. We had saved for furniture and the first payment for the car, but we also were saving for a down payment on a house for us and the baby. We had not needed this bit of bad luck.

Despite the difficulties, that spring of 1964 we began looking for a home although Ivan was the only one working. We found one house we liked, not in the old city but a little bit out, where we would have a garage and a yard. We felt the price wasn't too high for our budget, so our first home was 4341 Walker, in Kansas City, Kansas. We had two bedrooms, a living room, a large kitchen, a bathroom, a basement, and an attached garage. This was our castle, we thought! We won't ask for anything else. We worked with realtors for a price of $12,500, with a down payment of $2,500 and monthly payments of $95.00.

When we moved in, we struggled along on Ivan's small check till Simone was seven months old. Then I got a job in a sewing factory. Since we had only one car, Ivan took the baby to a sitter, then took me to work, then went to his own job. When the baby was sick, we had to reverse the procedure and take Simone to a doctor. Unfortunately, my work was to make uniforms, and the material had been treated with some chemical to which I was allergic. My ears began aching, then I struggled with breathing and poor blood circulation. I worked only four months there before I had to quit. Through the winter I stayed home, but returned in the spring, working there another four months. The baby cried every morning when we left her with the sitter, and that became too much for Ivan and me. The situation ended when we went to pick her up and found neither the sitter nor Simone there, although her husband and his friend were there playing cards. Her man said his wife would bring Simone to us later. We received a call from the sitter, stating that she had left her husband for good and was staying at her mother's in another part of town. She wanted to continue sitting Simone at her mother's house and promising to pick her up and bring her home. We said "no" to this arrangement.

Ivan comforted me: "Stay home, Ana. Take care of me, our baby and yourself. Make meals for all of us and I can come home in peace after a hard day's work." So I stayed home with Simone, managing our small budget to have enough for daily living and payments on our car and the house.

Later in that year, something unexpected and wonderful happened to me and my family: After five years in the court system, my inheritance from Uncle Matt was approved. I had almost forgotten about it. Those distant cousins had pushed for that inheritance clear to the Supreme Court, and they had lost all three times. My lawyer sent me the following letter:

"Dear Ana, I am reporting to you good news. Court is over and you should be the one who should be happy, because you are receiving $15,890.37. For my work, I will be paid $7,439, and your inheritance tax is $1,310.83. You and I should be happy all of this is over."

As Ivan was working, I called a taxi, took Simone and the bank documents for our loan on the house, and paid off the loan, depositing the money left over in our savings account. I didn't feel richer than I did before receiving that money, but I felt much more secure with our life in this new land. Ivan's paycheck now stretched further than it had before that money came to us.

In Croatia, my mother's sisters and their children were upset, saying the money should be theirs and not mine, because their relationships to Matt Brozenic were closer than mine. I had never asked Uncle Matt to leave any of his possessions to me. I had asked him only to help with papers so Ivan and I could immigrate to America. When he became ill, he left us something to help us start our lives here a little easier than it had been for him.

As the case wound through the courts, my parents had been having difficulties with mother's sisters and their children. One of my aunts had written me a letter in which she said, *"Dear Ana, not only you will be rich from Uncle Matt's money, but your entire family will also be rich when you will send them a portion of that money."*

Could anybody be rich who could buy one little house of five rooms? But people in the old country think in

America anybody who has a few thousand dollars is rich. Only we who have come to America know how little a few thousand dollars can buy here when one starts a new life with only one piece of luggage. I didn't have to share any of that money, but I did. I gave $500 to my mother and the same to each of her two sisters, and I sent my brothers $500 each.

That same year, Ivan and I attended classes, learning about the American Constitution and the country's history. The following year, on May 24, 1966, we became U.S. citizens and were proud to be able to say,

"We are Americans."

Chapter 14: **More New Experiences**

Most of us have a dream -- to accomplish something in our lives. My husband Ivan had often had that dream since he was a little boy growing up on his family's small farm. He wasn't satisfied with what his future would look like there. He told me how once after WWII some local communist authorities were driving by his family's field. Recognizing his father, they stopped to talk with him and Ivan. They remarked, "Juro, have you thought about giving your son a free education such as a machinist in Karlovac?" Ivan was all excited and went toward their car, but his father wasn't excited about letting his son be educated with communist ideas. When Ivan was eighteen years old, he went to Karlovac to work in a government factory. He did not want to take out the mandatory communist membership and listen to the propaganda. By 1965 Ivan could speak English and had his own car. He went searching for a job where he could learn to be a machinist. He found one in a factory named Darby *(An owner of that factory was Harry Darby, a former U.S. senator for the state of Kansas)*. There Ivan began learning his trade and was paid more than in his previous place. He had taken the first step toward the future he had set his mind to.

We had been successful in making our secret plan a reality, but one thing was still bothering me. Both my brothers and I had left my hard working parents alone on that small Brdo farm. They were getting older, and making a living for themselves had become even harder. Both of my brothers, Drago and Jure, lived in Croatian cities. They were having a hard time accomplishing enough for their own families' future. They couldn't take our parents in. Their homes were not even large enough for their own immediate families.

When Ivan and I asked my parents to come live with us, they were very happy. So, in July of 1967, like their own fathers many years before, my parents arrived in Kansas City. My father started to work soon after they came. He got a job in the same company where Ivan worked, although not on the big machines.

Ivan had asked for a job there even though he wasn't yet a good machinist. He pushed himself constantly. He said he studied so hard that his eyes got wet when the work wasn't as easy for him. Ivan was very tough. He wouldn't give up on accomplishing his objective, no matter how hard it was for him. The Intercontinental Company was owned by a man then over 90 years old. He was retired, but still came to see the place when he visited from California. He had emigrated from Germany many years before, starting the company with only one machine, which was still there. As Ivan's skill as a machinist improved, the owner would stop by his machine every time he came. Unlike the communist-owned companies in Yugoslavia, this factory gave Ivan all the opportunity he needed to advance.

When my parents came, they found many people who had come to Kansas City from Ribnik County. My parents knew their families even better than my husband and I did. This was a good beginning. All of us felt right at home among these familiar families.

My father found his brother, Marko Bosiljevac, who had married his wife Mary the same month and year as my father was born. The brothers had since seen each other only once in their lives, when Uncle Marko had visited us in Croatia. Father had one more sister in America. Her name was Ljube (Bosiljevac) Mlinaric. The oldest child in their family, she lived in Escanaba, Michigan. She and my father had never seen each other. She came with her daughter, her son-in-law and one son, Jure, to see my father when she was 81 years old.

My parents lived two years with us; then they rented the first floor of a house once owned by father's cousin, Franca Novosel, and her husband. My husband's grandfather, Stepan Fabac, had also lived in that house for more than twenty-five years before he decided to go home to his wife Mary and their only child, Ivan's mother Milka. The house was on Ann Avenue, right across from St. John Church, which Croatians had built at the beginning of the Twentieth Century. Next to the church was an orphanage run by nuns. After coming to this country, my mother worked there until she retired.

(Our son Brian below)

By 1970 I was feeling stronger, so Ivan and I decided to have another child. Our son Brian was born August 11, 1971. When Brian was about nine years old, we were invited to one of our friends' homes. Another family which we knew only from seeing them here and there were also invited. The parents' names were Loren and Helen Taylor, and their son David was with them. I found out that David was born in 1971. Curious, I asked Helen for the date, and she said, "August 11." Smiling, I told her, "These two boys were born on the same day. I have a clipping from the newspaper, and I will see if both of them are in that article. When I got home I looked it up. Sure enough, both Brian and David were listed, although David was born in Provident Hospital, Brian in Bethany.

One year after Brian's birth we started to look for a larger house with three bedrooms. When we couldn't find what we wanted, we looked in areas with good schools for a lot on which we could build. We couldn't have found one any closer, because the highschool was only 500 feet from our lot. We built the house in 1972. My parents were looking for a small house as well, so they bought our previous house. I still live in the home we built, and our children grew up there.

At last, like our Parisian friends, Ivan and I began taking some vacations. When Brian was two, we had our first trip with him and Simone. We had taken Simone with us to Canada twice and to the Ozarks a few times. This one was also in the Ozarks, but Brian was homesick. When we got to our small motel, Brian took Ivan's hand, pulling him to the door. I told Ivan, "Do as he wants you to do and we will see what he wants." Although Brian spoke very little by that age, he pulled his father clear to the car. Clearly he wanted to go home. Ivan comforted him, "We have to sleep here tonight, but tomorrow we will have a good time. You will like it." Brian was never too excited to be away from home. Simone was sad every time we returned from vacation, but Brian was happy. Like all children, ours had different personalities.

In 1974, seventeen years since we had left Grice, I was reunited with my brother Jure, who had come to see us and our parents. Ivan and I had feared returning to a communist country. Some, although not all, who had visited Yugoslavia after escaping were accused by the communists of espionage and were put in jail. Many people who had left parents, wives and children in Croatia during the first half of the twentieth century were never able to return to see their families.

One year before Jure came, my parents had visited Croatia. It was easier for them to return because they had left legally. Father and mother went to see the property on which they had lived for more than fifty years. Mother later said, "When I saw our property, so neglected, I had the feeling of wanting to return to

America that day if I could." I, too, have returned there in later years, and it was very painful to compare what I saw to what I remembered. When we lived in that village everything was clean, the grass was cut, the bushes and trees were trimmed. Our yards looked like some kind of park. When the people left, everything looked abandoned, which it really was.

When Brian was five and Simone twelve, we vacationed in Colorado. The children had never seen high mountains, but Ivan and I wanted to experience those again. Of course, we remembered our painful travel over mountains from Italy to France, but we also longed for the mountains we had grown to love when we lived in Grice. Brian, of course, had wanted to go home shortly after we got to Colorado, and we had to persuade him again that the next day we would visit high mountains and green valleys.

What a pleasure it was for me to enjoy again green valleys full of wild flowers and small streams. The beauty of the nature in the Rocky Mountains filled my heart with wonder again, as it had when I was a child in Brdo, admiring the majestic peaks on the Croatian-Slovenian border. Ivan and I also let the children choose what they wanted to do on that trip, including horseback riding. Ivan had ridden his family's horse, but this was a first experience for me *(See photo above)*. We also became prospectors behind Pike's Peak. I wasn't aware that there had been a gold mine there, but we did find traces of gold on small rocks, and took some for souvenirs.

Brian was ready for school when we returned home. Being so close to our house, the school was in easy walking distance for the children. The only drawback was that it was many years before I learned to drive a car. When I did, it was with difficulty. Ivan had great patience with his own work, but in teaching his wife how to drive, he lost it often. I had learned the meanings of road signs on my own, but I never told him that. When I was ready, I called a cab to pick Brian and me up for my trip to the license place. When Ivan came home, I showed him my driving permit. After one unsuccessful try, I got my license, although for a long time I wasn't very comfortable driving, especially out of our neighborhood.

Ivan and I had long planned to travel to the western United States, so in 1978 we bought a van and with our friends Joe and Millie Sambol, their daughter Dianne and our children, we headed west. We traveled through Oklahoma, New Mexico and Arizona before reaching California. Naturally, we took the children to Disney Land first. Next was Santa Catalina Island, then Hollywood before traveling to Las Vegas. After we parents visited some shows, we played the slot machines a little. Our next stop was Yellowstone Park, where I was surprised to see some snow still in the valley in July. We did enjoy touring the beautiful park, including viewing deer and bears.

After two weeks vacationing, we sped home to 'Brian's blue bike,' while Simone, as usual, kept saying "I don't want our vacation to end." To Ivan and me our new lives in America were, in a way, a constant 'vacation' -- being united with family and friends here, the joys of becoming parents and sharing with each other the freedom, wonders and experiences of living, working and traveling in our new country.

Chapter 15: **Ivan's Dream Comes True . . .**

The second half of the 1970's was good for small businesses. Ivan worked ten-hour days, six days a week, making good money with his overtime. President Jimmy Carter tried hard to create jobs and lower the government's deficit. Small businesses boomed as the economy improved. Many times during this decade Ivan hinted to me that he would like to go into business for himself but didn't have anybody to help him. By that time Ivan was a good machinist, and had talked with some coworkers about going with him in a machine shop of his own.

One day as I was changing my clothes after church, Ivan tried again softly to bring his dream to my attention. He brought up the name of one coworker I knew slightly and said, "Eddy would like to go with us into business." I found myself in the same situation as in 1957 when Ivan had wanted me to make the main decision of our lives – the one which would bring us to America. I really don't know which of those two decisions was harder to make. The one twenty-two years earlier had been sudden; there wasn't much time to think what to do. The one in 1979 had no sure answer. Because we were financially secure, it would have been easy for me to say, "No, we are not going into any kind of business." The idea, however, was appealing, but it wouldn't be simple. A machine shop would require a building, lots of equipment, coworkers and customers. I rarely originated such ideas because they frightened me, but when Ivan did, he seemed to think I had some kind of magic in me to make his dreams a reality. When Ivan pushed me to approve something, he knew that if I did approve, I would know how to implement it. So now I had to figure out how to keep from losing the money we had built up in savings.

Ivan invited Ed Weidler and his wife to our home to discuss going into business together. Like Ivan, Ed was a good machinist. He was American-educated. I had taken some English classes when we came to the U.S., but Ivan hadn't. He did know how to speak English, and could read but not write well. I was still home with the children, but I did have a desire to do something additional with my time and could, perhaps, be useful to the men. The agreement to go into business together was made. As Ivan and Ed were working long hours, they had no time to look for a lot to buy, so they asked me to do that. I found a house for $2,500 on a lot 38'x125'. That was enough room for us to build a 30'x80' building. Ed said, "We don't have the money to pay for one-half of that lot, but we will give it to you when we have saved the money.

They could not, however, save any money in the near future, so after two months they said they would have to give up the plan. We had let Ed and his wife put their names on that property deed, which was our first mistake. There were to be others as we went on with our plan. We had them sign a quit-claim deed, which they did. We tried to avoid any mistakes which would cause us to lose our savings. I calculated that if we couldn't go on with our plan, we could sell our building and recover our investment.

Little by little then, more decisions fell on my shoulders. Whatever needed to be done, I did. Well, through my life I have kept my mind busy; otherwise I would get bored. At least now I was driving, which made taking care of many details easier. In March of 1979 I found a company to demolish that old house for $750, and Ivan and I talked of plans to build our business on that spot. Originally he had said, "If I have a building just as large as a good garage, I would be happy," but when we planned in reality, Ivan changed his mind. First he said he wanted 30'x40' for the building, but when we were ready to make drawings, he wanted 30'x80' – a size of building not suitable for our budget. Ivan, however, was persistent as usual. He wanted me to "swing my magic stick" and get him what he wanted.

It took very careful planning, and I was able to get people who had done such jobs before. As Ivan continued working long hours, he came by only long enough to tell me how to tell the builders what to do. As construction began, we had enough money to put the shop under a roof. As I had told Ivan in the beginning, we got into trouble with not enough funds for a building that size. We could have borrowed money from the bank, but that wasn't my plan. I wanted to pay cash for the building and borrow money for the machinery. We could afford that even if we didn't have much business at the beginning.

Two years after we had built our own house, we had also bought the adjacent lot. A small, older house on that lot was in poor shape, and we had planned to demolish it someday and build a new home for my parents. Now, at a dead end for extra money, we had to do something to continue with our plan. We decided to sell that house, but my parents wouldn't let us do that. Instead, they loaned us $18,000 to continue with our building. That left us still about $10,000 short for what we needed to finish the shop and put a down payment on machinery. We refinanced our old, small house and borrowed $10,000, which was enough. The new shop building was completed by the end of 1979. At least, we then had a little breathing space to think about what to do next.

Ivan knew how to make the business function, but we needed to take care of the legal requirements. That was when we decided to consult a lawyer. He started our incorporation papers on February 28, 1980. I brought a bunch of books from the library and learned how to prepare the papers and what to do with them. We needed to borrow money for machinery at the worst time ever, when the interest rate was at 18%. We borrowed $30,000 with which Ivan bought three machines for our company. Reluctant to depend only on our new business to provide enough income, Ivan worked another entire year at his old company. Although we knew we were in for more difficulties, I never said "Why did we get into this?" to Ivan or to myself. I had confidence in both of us that we would work it out as we always had.

On our $30,000 loan, our monthly payments were $661, which was about the amount of Ivan's weekly check. At least, I thought, even if we had no business at all, we would not lose more money while waiting for the situation to improve. With that 18% interest rate, business had slowed down all over, but we hoped for that to change the following year.

It was a frightening time for us. When we finished the building and bought three machines, all we had left in the bank was $40 and Ivan's weekly salary. I often thought, was it harder in Paris when we arrived there with no money? Or was it harder when we had property worth good money and other property which wasn't ours and no money in savings? Although our business was not providing any income, it did entail expenses. Then, in 1981 we got $6,000 in a tax refund which we hadn't expected. I continued to talk with some local businesses to give us contracts, and Ivan, never afraid of hard work, took on those after he came from his regular job.

Then one day I hit the jackpot! I visited a company just one block from our shop. A young man who was giving out work said to me, "Look," as he lifted a whole bunch of drawings up, "do you think your husband could work on this?" I explained to him what kind of machines we had and said, "I am certain Ivan can do that." When he brought the drawings to Ivan, my husband assured him he could do most of the work. Finally Ivan was able to quit his old job and start to work for his own company.

Inflation was not getting lower, but our work was going well. Later in 1980 we were able to refinance our payments at 15%, which helped some. We paid off our first machines in seven years.

We named our shop "Wyandotte Machine Shop, Inc." after the name of the county where we lived. The first man we hired was Dan Earley, whom Ivan knew well. Both of them were good machinists. They did quality work and made good money. First, we paid off my parents' loan; then we bought more machines.

Simone graduated from high school in 1982 while we were still struggling with our finances. That, however, didn't stop us from sending our daughter to college forty miles away, at the University of Kansas in Lawrence. I felt I was leaving one part of myself in that town because I had been with the children day and night since they were born. However, during my entire life I had wished for a better education than I had, so my husband and I were glad to give Simone this opportunity. My education had died in Grice and Ivan's in Karlovac. This had been true also of many bright young people in our country when war and then communism didn't permit us to get ahead. Ivan and I had sacrificed mostly so that our children would have the opportunity for higher education that we had not had.

By 1984 our business was doing fine, but as Billy Graham once said, "When things in my life are going well, then God comes to slap me in the face to calm me down." During the spring, I watched a talk show on which a lady doctor advised ladies to occasionally check their breasts for a tumor. I did that right away and was stunned to feel a lump on the edge of my right breast. My doctor said she would make an appointment for my X-ray as soon as possible.

After my biopsy, the surgeon had me come to his office to hear the results. While I had waited for the results, it had never clicked in my mind that I could really have cancer. I just wouldn't let myself think of that. I drove myself to his office.

When the doctor and his nurse came into that small room, he wasted no time telling me that I did, indeed, have cancer. Cold waves streamed through me from my feet to the top of my head. The doctor showed no sadness on his face, which gave me an even worse time, as he said, "Are you OK?" "I am not sure," I responded.

Pulling myself together, I drove home on I-70 during heavy traffic, wondering if I could get home safely in such a condition. More than anything else, I wondered how to tell my children. How could I die and leave them without me? The whole family depended on me – the children, my husband who couldn't take care of his new business alone, and my parents who had nobody but me to care for them.

When I arrived home, Simone, now twenty, asked me what the doctor said. I started to cry, telling her and Brian, thirteen, that I had cancer. Ivan arrived home to find all three of us crying. Nobody was able to eat that night. From that evening, Ivan and I didn't talk of anything for many days but what was very important. We had planned to attend the wedding of Stanly and Kristin Stancic's daughter that weekend, but we were too upset even to tell them why we didn't attend. *(It would be 1995 before I would have the chance to explain to Kristina why we weren't there. Telling her finally took a heavy weight from my mind.)*

The doctors removed my tumor and some surrounding tissue. Then I took radiation treatments. They said I had an 80% chance of survival, but I was still afraid of a recurrence. I was lucky not to lose my breast, and am even more lucky to be in this world so long after. It's

226

funny, but I never talk about the cancer with any of my family. We just can't talk about painful things in the past. I am grateful that God, once again, pulled me out of a real difficulty.

I thought to do something for all of us, so I planned a trip. We traveled in our van to South Carolina, then all over Florida, even Key West. One day, going north through swampy territory by the gulf, we stopped at a park to eat. Suddenly I noticed that all of our hands and legs were black, covered in hordes of the largest mosquitoes we had ever seen. I yelled, "Wipe them off and run for the van. They will eat us alive!" We closed it up and drove fast from that place! We kept looking for a nice beach, and found the perfect one in Pensacola – on a tiny island covered with sand that looked like baby powder, surrounded by beautiful blue water, truly clean and clear. We were having a wonderful time until I heard that hurricane David was coming from the gulf. Although it was 200 miles away, the waves on our beach began to get much higher, so I suggested we leave and move inland, which was disappointing to the family. For many years after Brian said, "You ruined my vacation when you forced us to leave that beautiful beach." I hadn't thought that would mean so much to him.

We reached Memphis, Tennessee close to dark. We discovered that the next day marked the anniversary of Elvis Presley's death, and the town was full of fans. Elvis had been my favorite singer, too. His voice was distinctive, and his songs touched everyone. We were very lucky to get two rooms at the Hilton due to the kindness of a lady at another hotel. We needed to get home, however, so we left the next day, only to drive into the remnants of the very hurricane we had run from in Florida. I started driving from Memphis, but I had a hard time seeing as tropical rain began pouring down on us. I had ruined another day of Brian's vacation, but it was nice to arrive home, finding everything as we had left it.

No longer do I have to try to take
apples from neighbors' yards.
I enjoy picking and eating these
from my own back yard in Kansas City.

Chapter 16: . . . and So Does Mine!

We had never been back to our homeland in Croatia, which we had fled twenty-nine years before. Now, our business continued to do well despite the difficult economy. However, it had been only one year since my cancer surgery, so I wanted to fulfill this other dream just in case the worst happened to me. The trip had to be special for our children, so in 1986, just after the new year began, I asked Ivan and the children if they wanted to take this journey with me. It would not be a simple trip, because I wanted the family to see where Ivan and I had spent those years trying to get to America -- to see Paris and Italy and to travel the road we had followed from Croatia to Paris.

We would have to leave our business in the hands of our employees, but Ivan, who was a wonderful husband and father, never complained when I said that everything would be fine. I asked him if he would be willing to rent a van in Germany and drive it through Europe. Ivan gave me permission to gather information and prepare all the details. We would leave in June, 1986, and I paid for the trip in March. Between then and June, though, something happened which made proceeding with our plans difficult. Word of terrorism in Rome and radiation spreading across Europe from the explosion of the Chernoble nuclear reactor was frightening enough for some people to cancel visits to Europe, but we decided to go ahead.

Reaching New York, we boarded the plane for our overseas flight, but as we awaited liftoff, we saw mechanics on the wings of the plane. Shortly we were told to get off because that plane needed repairs. We boarded another plane, not to Munich, Germany, but to Zurich, Switzerland. Another passenger reassured us, saying, "This is nothing new. It happens every evening at the New York airport. I knew that because a travel agent who is a friend of mine warned me about that." He continued, "That is capitalism; various companies work together to save money during this crisis time when people cancel their trips."

When we arrived in Zurich the next morning, nobody knew how to get us to Munich, so we waited hours in that airport without help. Finally some people called their agents to take care of us, and eventually an airplane from Germany arrived. We were flown to Munich, arriving at our hotel close to dark. The next morning we continued another long ride to Paris, arriving in the late afternoon.

(View of the Avenue des Champs Elysees)

Because of the terrorism threat, we expected difficulties crossing European borders, but our German van enabled us to continue through the German-French border without being stopped. Simone and Brian kept asking when we would arrive in Paris, and I replied, "When you see many electrical lines, we will be close. That was how dad and I knew when we first arrived in Paris." Our highway led straight into the middle of a typically large Paris traffic jam, much greater than any had been when we lived there. Our young people were stunned, as was

I. When cars jammed in the middle of the city, drivers just blew their horns till the police came to regulate traffic. When we finally got out of that jam we turned into smaller streets to avoid that kind of situation.

We remembered how hard it had been to get a permanent place to stay, but we didn't realize that it would be equally hard to get hotel rooms. Avoiding some trashy places, we asked at some hotels, but nothing was available. It was almost dark when we stopped between some buildings to decide what to do. We spotted a young lady walking toward us. In German she asked if we needed help; when we said that we were Americans, she then spoke English. She took me to one hotel right around the corner. The man said that

he didn't have empty rooms but he would call other hotels in their chain. He found one on another street which was easy for Ivan to find. We even found one parking space left on the street in front of the hotel. Afraid we wouldn't be as lucky again, we didn't move the van during our stay there.

(The same spot I had taken Ivan's picture 28 years earlier. See photo on p. 175.)

The next day we began taking our young people to see main attractions of Paris, as well as one of those places Ivan and I had lived in Paris – 7 Passage Legendre. I took a picture of that building where we had lived on the second and third floors. After two days running from one place to another, it wasn't enough to show the children everything.   We met one family we had known in those days in Paris; that was Denica Doricic and her daughter Mirjana.   We didn't get to see Danica's husband Ivan, who was visiting his family in Croatia, but the ladies took us to a nice restaurant and prepared a nice lunch at their house the next day. After we ate, we walked in their garden where they had fruit trees and vegetables. Danica told us her brother John Rehoric and his wife Ana had immigrated to Kansas City, but were no longer living.

We were able to stay in Paris only three days, leaving on Saturday for Nice, where Ivan and I had stayed one full day waiting for the train which took us to Paris. Our hotel was in an ideal location, away from the traffic noise on the boulevard by the ocean. There European cars roared day and night. We stayed two days to see that enchanting place on the French Riviera, strolling through the little city with its cozy restaurants and old fashioned stores. We also went to the beach, but it was nothing like the ones in Florida with their soft sand and warm water.

We passed through Monaco and arrived in Manton where we had slid down a winding road from the mountains as we crossed the Italian/French border with Franc Cokel and his father. I wished we could have gone on the same road through those mountains to repeat our life journey but we couldn't afford enough time to walk. We couldn't take the winding roads we had traveled by bus because by this time the highway was built through the mountains. When we arrived in the little town of Pisa, we drove right to its main attraction, the Leaning Tower. We shouldn't have taken the one-way street there, because a policeman told Ivan to return on another street. Simone, Brian and I got out of the van, and Ivan said he would turn back on another street. He took my purse and everything else in the van, so we had nothing with us, no documents, no money. We waited and waited, but Ivan didn't return, and I started to panic. What if somebody had robbed him? What if police had arrested him for driving on the wrong street? He couldn't even speak Italian. Even at the information booth by the Leaning Tower, nobody spoke English. As I tried to explain our problem to a policeman, I finally spotted Ivan coming. He said he couldn't turn back till he crossed the river and wandered around the city to find one street on his left. From this experience we learned to stay together no matter where we went.

Because of the delay in Pisa, it was nearly dark before we reached Rome and looked for a hotel. A group of young people pushed one young man forward, telling us he speaks English. He took us around the corner and showed us a hotel there where we were able to find rooms. Those young people reminded Ivan and me of our experience with the friendly and helpful Italians when we crossed the Yugoslav/Italian border and the nice lady on a hill who had given us cookies and tea before we turned to the mountains.

We still had three more weeks to see our family and the country in which we had been born. We were uneasy about facing communists, even after that long a time, since we had left illegally. Others who had gone back had told us that rarely did the communists bother people like us. Even after all these years, Ivan was particularly nervous as we approached the border with Yugoslavia. At the border, the police came to check us, peeking into the van to see if we had brought any contraband. Their eyes were attracted by our new video cameras which we had bought just before we left on our trip. The guards smiled and said to Ivan, Come with us to our office. We will take the serial number and style of camera so you won't have problems taking it out of our country.

Ivan followed them, but he was scared that they would do more than just look at his camera. Because of our German van, they had originally thought we were German, but when they looked at our passports, they said, "Oh, you are our people." They asked us what we had in our van besides the camera, and we told them,

"Just our clothes and gifts for our families." Much to our relief, they then said we were free to continue our trip.

Our first stop was in the city of Ljubljana, Slovenia, where my brother Jure lived with his wife Ana, daughter Jadranka and Son Marko.

Jure had visited us in Kansas City in 1974, but we were meeting the rest of his family for the first time. Our children speak English and Croatian, while their children speak Slovenian and Croatian. In the beginning Simone and Brian were afraid their Croatian was not good enough for their cousins to understand. After a bike ride together, Brian and Marko returned with good communication.

(Jure's son Marko, left, and daughter Jadranka, right.)

After a few days, we were on our way to Karlovac where my brother Drago lived with his wife Ana and a son Kruno, who is only two months older than Brian. Ivan's sister Ljube with her family also lived in Karlovac. When we entered Ribnik County, I could hardly wait to return to Grice. As we approached the bridge over the Kupa River, I asked Ivan which river that was. It seemed to me so small, and the sign on the Slovenian side was Kulpa, so I didn't recognize it. In the van we passed everything so fast I couldn't believe how close to each other those places were. I had never seen them from a car. We had always walked from place to place.

(Right: Simone and Ivan's niece Ivanka on Brdo with our rented German van.)

Finally we were close to Grice where Ivan's brother Drago and his family lived. Mostly older people lived in the village where Ivan was born, but there were some younger folks also. We didn't recognize some of those people with whom we had been friends, nor they us. Then we were on our way to my Brdo. It was most important to me to see that hill and the old house where I had been born. It was about a ten-minute walk from Jarmek's Valley to Brdo. When I arrived at my yard, I remembered how that had been my park, my Garden of Eden, with all kinds of fruit for us to eat through the summer. That yard didn't look like that now, because nobody lived there anymore. However, my brothers still came there to take care of the house and yard, so it didn't look as bad as it might have. The house was amazingly well preserved. There was no smell of damp because the house was built of solid woods and over a basement. My brothers sometimes were going there for picnics and sometimes cooked meals in that old fashioned stove.

In Grice we met many people who had grown up with us, as well as some who were much older than we were. However, some people had died during the time we were gone; many of the younger people left, as we had, to their cities or to different countries. I noticed particularly that the liveliness I remembered was missing in the village. As we passed by in our van, no people or animals were on those fields. We had worked the fields through each summer in order to have crops ready for the rest of the year. I wondered now, what are those few families going to eat if they don't prepare their crops? I found out that most of these families had at least one member working in Germany; therefore they had plenty of money to buy their food from farmers with more fertile land.

I would have liked to stay longer in Brdo, but the house wasn't prepared for sleeping in it, so we had to sleep at my brother's house in Karlovac. The following weekend, though, we went back for a picnic with our family and some friends. We had a wonderful time walking through that nice yard and even walked to the forest which isn't too far from the house. That day I will remember my entire life.

One week we went to the Adriatic Croatian oceanside, where the whole family had a wonderful time. Our three weeks in Croatia flew by fast, however, and it was time to return home to our business and our American lives. The trip had been wonderful for us, but even more memorable for our children. Brian and Simone had the chance to see what their parents' lives had been like before we arrived in Kansas City. That had been my dream for a long, long time. It had happened thanks to my husband who agreed to take that trip, and who always did what he could to fulfill his family's dreams. My parents had anxiously waited for our return. They had handled overseeing our business, our employees, and our house as well for the five weeks we were gone

The late 1980's were good years. We bought a few more machines and two buildings adjacent to our business property. Business was great – not too large for us to handle, and not too small. Everything in our business and in our private property was paid off. Only my health still concerned me.

In 1987, Simone met a young man at a dance organized by the Catholic Society for single people. Dean Haverkamp had been born and raised in Seneca, KS. Like Simone, he also worked at the Kansas University Medical Ctr., although they hadn't known each other before. They married on

July the 9th, 1988. I made dresses for Simone and all of the four bridesmaids: Nancy Jadric, Ann Cavlavic, Angela Zeleznjak & Maid of Honor, Kristina Hutujac.

(Above, right: Ivan and I, Simone & Dean, Brian.)

Dean's parents, Bill and Patricia Haverkamp, as well as other friends and relatives of the groom arrived, of course. My brother Jure and his family came to the wedding, and my brother Drago's son Kruno came with them. Simone's friend Mirjana Doricic came from Paris. Drago's daughter, Mira Bolibruch, flew in from Hamilton Canada with her little daughter Natasha, and my cousin Ana Drgastin, her husband Ivan and daughter Nedeljke from Kitchener, Canada.

Our house was full for a few days, but I was still young enough to take care of everything and everybody. The wedding took place in Krist the King Church, followed by a reception for about 250 guests representing families and friends of the couple.

(Simone on right enjoys a visit with Jadranka, Jure's daughter, on the balcony of Jure's home in Slovenia.)

Chapter 17: **Croatia Is Reborn**

For Europe, 1989 was an incredible year. Communism was crumbling. We had never witnessed such history as we did after World War II when Europe split – the eastern part to communism and the western to democracy. Even normally stoic people became emotional then. We who emigrated for western democracies had reason to be relieved and happy. We had chosen to leave our countries because of the communists' repressive policies. We watched what seemed to us unbelievable -- the fall of the Berlin Wall which the Russians had erected in 1961 to divide the city of Berlin and split the east to communism and the west to democracy. We knew that it would take a long and painful process to end the hard concrete mentality that ruled communists' minds. I personally thought that would never end, because I saw how they had spread their poison in the minds of people under their control. Even though I was young when I lived there, I still was aware of those who stuck with the communists no matter how wrong they were. My mother once said to her younger sister Milka, whose husband was a communist, "Milli, how can you stick with them when you know how unfair they are to people not in favor of their ideas?" She replied, "Mara, we know they are unfair, but we still love them."

Some Croatians who believed in communistic ideas left, as we did, because communists didn't create better lives for them, but still, the love of communism hadn't been erased from their systems. One of their sympathizers told my father, right here in Kansas City, "I can't help myself. Communism won't get out of my system no matter how hard I try." That man had lived in this country for years when he made that statement. He had enjoyed all the privileges of democracy, but his mind was still poisoned. In democratic countries people are free to go into any line of work they are able to handle; but in the country we had left, we couldn't, no matter how smart we were. Should someone start a small business, the communists would impose such high taxes on that business that it would collapse.

Despite the economic fall in Eastern Europe, communism didn't just evaporate from those minds which had been poisoned. Their countries had and will continue to have a difficult time adjusting to democracy; so, until young minds get more mature and take over the countries, the old will continue to live in that cocoon of false trust.

All over the world, we Croatian people waited for the moment when something new would happen in that combined country of Yugoslavia. Communism was not the only enemy to be defeated: In individual states there were also various nationalities which needed to become independent – free from occupation by those who had repressed Croatia for many years. Croatia had been suppressed by foreigners for 888 years, and for all of those centuries the Croatian people had yearned to get back their country.

When the Soviet Union fell apart, then the Yugoslav states had their chance. Those of us outside the country ached to see Croatians leaving their homes with only bags of their possessions in their hands. Later they found out that the Serbs had burned many of the beautiful homes they had left behind. The Serbian and Yugoslav army had occupied one-third of Croatia, and all Croatians in that part of the country became refugees in camps all over other parts of Croatia and in some other European countries. Those who chose to stay, suffering under communism, couldn't fight alone. We who had left for better conditions had a duty to help them, so we sent food to those who had lost everything.

How painful it was for Jasna Jadric, living here in Kansas City, to watch a television broadcast and recognize in a group of refugees her mother pushing a wheelbarrow containing her own old mother! Jasna's mother had lived in Vukovar, which was destroyed in 1991. A few months later, Jasna's mother, Ana Macan, left her mother with some relatives and came to her daughter to recover her strength. Gathered together in a Croatian hall to hear Ana Macan's horror story, most of us soon had tear-filled eyes. She told us how several people had hidden in one small basement for several months until the Yugoslav army took over the whole city and found them. When Croatia finally became independent, the government built houses little by little for those whose

homes had been destroyed. So, after ten years, Ana Macan went back to Vukovar to the small house which the Croatian government had built for her.

In every war, people who are sacrificed are not only from one side, but from both sides. When Croatians took back the part of their country which had been occupied, it was the Serbian people who left, fearing the Croatian army. Many of them had not wanted to wage war on us either; they needed to work on their own farms and feed their families, but their leaders were a greedy group who wanted to keep control in their hands. That is how it has always been . . . and how it will continue to be. Like most Americans who had come from Croatia, I watched and listened as I kept myself busy with our business, family and Croatian politics.

In the early 90's, Yugoslavia crumbled little by little, just like the Soviet Union. For Croatia, however, it wasn't as easy to break away as it was for the Slovenian state. Croatians had elected President Franjo Tudman to lead them, but that irritated Belgrade's central government. Two states out of six had declared independence; Croatia and Slovenia on June 25, 1991. That triggered wider war in both states. Trouble in Slovenia diminished soon after it started because Slovenia had only a small percentage of Serbians who would fight, but in Croatia, it was another story.

The big powers of the world decided the futures for small countries: America, France and England had not approved separation of Yugoslavia into individual states. Those big powers enjoy their own freedoms, but when it came to those under repression by other nations, they were not in favor of letting them choose for themselves. President George H.W. Bush sent his Secretary of State, James Baker, to Belgrade to give the Yugoslav government support for keeping the country together. Being in contact with leaders in Croatia, our people in North America organized a demonstration in Washington, D.C. to let President Bush and other politicians know how much we supported the independence of Croatia. In July, 1991, eighteen of us from Kansas City, Kansas, headed to the capital city. I was one of this group. For a day and half the night we traveled in three cars and one van to get within one hundred miles of our destination. We slept till morning, then arriving in Washington to join thousands of Croatian people from all over the United States and Canada for a peaceful demonstration. Many senators and representatives in Congress helped us with their speeches. One was Senator Bob Dole of Kansas, a major supporter for Croatia.

All day long the speeches continued until mid afternoon when we slowly marched to the White House, holding Croatian and American flags and signs asking President Bush to support Croatian independence. Already too many citizens had left Croatia. We wanted those remaining to have their own country, to build their own future for their children and future generations. Those of us who emigrated are happy to be where we are, but we still have strong feelings of support for those still in Croatia.

Traveling in the van with Joe and Carol Zugecic and a few others, I was pleased to be there for our Croatian cause, but also interested to see our U.S. capital. We took pictures and videos from everything we saw -- of the American and Croatian flags flickering over our shoulders and of each other in front of

the White House and the United States Capitol. *(The color photo on this book's front cover shows me holding a Croatian flag in the center.)*

This is America where we can do such things; in the country we came from, which at that time was Yugoslavia, we could not have done so. If we had, we would have found ourselves in jail soon after. In 1951 when my husband's sister was getting married, we carried the Croatian flag as we took the ride to the groom's house. Passing by a police station, we were stopped and asked why we carried that flag. The groom said, "We are carrying the Croatian flag because we are Croatian nationality. This is the kind of flag we use." The police said we should use a Yugoslav flag. They took ours and said to pick it up when we came back.

What a contrast to that incident our demonstration in Washington had provided! People in Washington noted that our demonstration had been peaceful and clean. They said we were the cleanest thousands of people they had ever had there. Our leaders had asked us to pick up all the trash we saw thrown on the ground and we did, because it isn't our Croatian way to trash the place where we stay.

We had enjoyed our trip, especially meeting other countrymen and finding out where they had come from. There were some whom we knew who now lived in other cities and Canada. We traveled all night long and the next day until we arrived back home, all tired and sleepy. The trip had been a good experience for us, and an exhausting one. Had it helped our Croatian cause or not? We had done our part to show the world how our people needed their own country, one in which every Croat would be proud to say, "I am (or my ancestors were) from the country of Croatia *(Hrvatske)* – a real country we have waited 888 years for." During the course of our history some Croatian people had said they came from Austria and sometimes from Hungary, and at least one, we came from Yugoslavia. The truth is, we didn't come from any of those countries. Those who came were just occupiers of Croatia.

Finally, on January 15, 1992, the European Union recognized Croatia and sent United Nations peace keepers to those parts of the country which had the biggest problems.

During this time of confusion in my homeland, there was also a long-standing confusion in my private life, as well. The difficulty centered around the inheritance I had received from Uncle Matt Brozenic some years before. I had exchanged letters with my Aunt Barbara and her daughter Ruzica for twenty years. The two of them were living in Karlovac with no relatives from the countryside to help them. Aunt Barbara and her daughter, who had a husband and a son, were in greater need of help than any other member of my mother's family.

Ever since I had received that money, my mother's entire family despised me, even though giving the money to me had been Uncle Matt's own idea. Still, I had helped my Aunt Barbara through the years before she died, but to her daughter Ruzica it was never enough. Being naturally soft hearted, the family friction tortured me inside. I began to think and think until finally I reached a decision. That money had come to me at the right time, when Ivan and I were coming to America. Our first wages were small, and we wanted to start building a family. The money from Uncle Matt had been a blessing. Now, Ivan and I were in good shape financially, and we were able to help our children as well. To give Uncle Matt's money away wouldn't hurt us, but it might stop mother's family's bickering and allow me to live a normal life. I decided to give away all of Uncle Matt's money including the interest it had earned. That would make me free. I couldn't give only Ruzica her part; I would have to give to all of mother's sisters or their children, deducting only what I had already given them over the years. I gave mother her share, which she gave to my two brothers. Ivan was not happy with my decision, but he agreed that we had enough. God had been good to us, and through our hard work we had built a solid foundation for our lives.

That fall of 1992 Ivan and I visited our relatives in Croatia to see what they were going through. In Karlovac, where my brother and his family and Ivan's sister and her family lived, the war had been really bad. Although none of them had suffered personal loss, the entire country had suffered devastation which affected every person living there. Karlovac was full of refugees from surrounding areas and from Bosnia. With my video camera, I captured pictures of many destroyed homes and refugees at the city market where farmers used to sell their produce. The refugees were waiting for the Croatian authorities to find them homes in buildings which had been used as army barracks for the Yugoslav army. I asked the refugees where they had come from. "From the camp named Manjaca," they told me. Then I remembered how I had seen a picture in a newspaper of one fragile, bony bodied man who was in that camp. I asked if they knew where he was and they replied, "He is in Zagreb in a hospital."

Never, I had thought, in Yugoslav territory would there be any kind of war again. I believed that people in Europe had become civilized enough to solve their problems peacefully. I was wrong.

Our visit to Croatia hadn't only been sad. It had also been nice to see our families.

(Left photo: Drago's son Kruno and wife Alenka Bosiljevac. Right photo: Drago's daughter Mira and Branko Bolibruch from Canada.)

Also, we had visited places to which we had sent things for refugees. At the city hall in Karlovac, news media waited for us and ran with a tape to Zagreb in time to have us on the evening news. They had learned of my work in Kansas on behalf of their refugees.

Both of my brothers with their wives joined Ivan and me in visiting Zagreb. Drago was anxious to know if his old visa (from the early '70's) to come to America was still good. At the American embassy, I explained how he would work in our machine shop and would live with our parents in Kansas City.

The lady looked up his file and said, "His visa is still waiting for him after all these years. He can go as soon as you send a letter guaranteeing his work and living place." When we got home I sent that paper, and my brother was in Kansas City just three months later.

(Above: Both brothers with me in back; our parents in front. Photo below: When Drago arrives in America,

Ivan shows him how his machine works.)

It was also nice to have another member of our family

with us. In 1994, my other brother Jure, came to visit. That was the first time for us and our parents to be reuni-ted since Ivan and I had left Croatia in 1957.

We had certainly picked the right season to return to Croatia. It was our wonderful fall season when the special harvest had come in. Chestnuts were ready for harvest, so Ivan and I picked up some and roasted them for our enjoyment. It was also mushroom season, which Drago helped us pick and his wife prepared for us. Grapes were in abundance, and my brother had some although he lives in the city. These sights, sounds and tastes brought my childhood delights flooding back, and again my heart sang with love for those memories.

We also took a trip to Slovenia where Jure and his family lived. The most beautiful place there is Lake Bled and the lush nature that surrounds it. The time then came for us to return home, a home in Kansas City where our closest family waited for us and we were filled with anticipation to see them, too.

In 1995 we celebrated two important family occasions: January 8th Ivan and I celebrated our 40th wedding anniversary and also my mother's 80th birthday, which was two days later. She said, "Nobody in my family lived to be 80, so I'm happy to have lived this long." At the time, she had no idea that she had a large tumor on her pancreas. For some time she had complained of an uncomfortable feeling in her stomach, but she had mentioned her stomach pain before, which she thought was an inflammation that she had learned to live with. Suddenly at the end of February she became ill again. Her doctor found something hard close to her stomach, and at the hospital, doctors saw a clear picture of the tumor. Because the cancer had already spread to her liver, they said there was nothing they could do to save her, and they pressed me to tell her the condition of it. That was the hardest moment of my life. Only one month later, on March 27, 1995, mother died. That was

248

the first death in our close family since her mother, Magdalena Jagas, died in 1956.

As difficult as it is for loved ones, death is as much a part of our lives as is birth. Simone was expecting her first baby that same year, and at least my mother knew of the pregnancy although she never saw the baby. Amanda was born June 26, 1995.

(Ivan's and my first grandchild, Amanda Haverkamp, daughter of Dean and Simone.)

Before her daughter's birth Simone had been working with me in the office at our machine shop. With the responsibility for her new child, however, she had to leave me alone to do all of the office work. This was a heavy load for me, but we had never employed anyone from outside of our family to take care of paper work in the business, so I had no plans to hire anyone now. Ivan had retired one year earlier, and Brian replaced him in the machine shop. Our son had finished his college courses, graduating with a degree as a Mechanical Engineer. Between terms he had already worked with the other machinists, but it was difficult for a man younger than any of his employees to be in charge for the first time. Some of the employees began to give us difficulties because they knew we needed them.

Throughout my life God has given me periodic difficulties. There must be a reason for that, and the mid 90's brought me plenty of anguish. I often thought of a quote my grandma used: "Dear God, Up in the sky is high and down on the earth is hard. I don't know where to turn." *("Dragi Boze, Gore je visoko, Dole je tvrdo, neznam kud cu se okrenut.")* Well, I came to that point on July 18, 1995. As I left for work that day, Ivan was still in bed, as he enjoyed sleeping late.

Ivan and I owned a small, older house next door which we had demolished to build a new home for my father. That morning, July 18th, the builders were still there when Ivan waved through his window for them to come in our house. Luckily he was able to open the door. One of the builders came to the window but didn't see Ivan again. He decided to come in and found Ivan lying on the floor, not moving or talking. The man called an ambulance and called me. The ambulance was still with Ivan when I got home. At the hospital the doctor informed us that Ivan had suffered a stroke. He spent three weeks in the hospital. Trying to keep up with the office work and overseeing the construction of the new house, I still managed to visit Ivan twice a day while he was there.

Brian was struggling with shop employees who took advantage of our situation when we needed their help the most. As Ivan's illness stabilized, I spent some time checking up on the office. Brian and I compared notes and found a situation we didn't like. When Simone came to a meeting with Brian and me, we decided to end the harassment, even though we knew that our biggest customers would leave us when we reduced our work force.

I had taught my children to be honest, whether it helps or hurts them in life. Brian was only 24 years old and new to the problems of running a business, and I was a woman in the male world of business. I had to stand up to our employees, showing them that this business is mine, and I am in charge of it. I had learned what freedom and opportunity meant in America, so I replaced my husband in our business. Fortunately, all of our customers knew me very well, and our business was able to survive. Although young and inexperienced, Brian was courageous, taking great responsibilities into his hands as he worked and led the activity in our machine shop. His greatest advantage was his engineering degree which his father had always wished for, himself.

Little by little the situation normalized in our business. With extensive therapy, Ivan was recuperating well. His right side was almost normal. Although his hand and leg were weaker, he could walk well, and his speech was showing good results, as well. We could only say, "Thanks be to God."

As our struggles lessened and we achieved stability in our own lives, we rejoiced too, in what our homeland had been able to achieve. The Croatian people had gotten their independence after centuries of struggle against foreign occupation. The destruction in that part of their country which the Serbs had occupied was, however, predominantly high. Too many homes had been demolished; too many schools and churches were destroyed.

I had been very young during World War II, but I had seen and felt what my people were going through. Ivan and I had left twelve years after that war, but the situation hadn't improved in all those years. Those of us who live out of Croatia have tried to help our people as much as we could. I have given many hours of work volunteering and donating money to help refugees who had lost their homes.

I am grateful to be an American, but I am also still grounded in my original homeland, my historic roots. (*It has been difficult for us to keep our nation's heritage through nine centuries of occupation. Even the true name of our country – Hrvatska -- is unfamiliar to people in much of the world. "Croatia" is a nickname* derived from the unusual neckware of our uniformed guards when we were under French rule centuries ago. The French called the guards "croats," from the French for cravats, and the name stuck.) Today, we Croatian people, whether still living there or not, are proud to have been a small part of achieving the independence of Croatia.

"We are not from Hungary, Austria or Yugoslavia. We are Croatians, from the country of Croatia" (Hrvatska).

Chapter 18: **Life's Circular Journey**

The year 2000 opened an exciting era in world history, the ending of the second millennium and the beginning of the third. It was a touching moment for those of us who lived to witness the promise of a better future.

By 2004, however, the television news in America had become depressing with constant wars, terrorism, criminal activities and everyone's worries over the deficit in our government's budget. As we watched satellite news from Croatia, all of those disturbing things were on their news, as well. One enjoyable moment came, however: On April 30, 2004, ten European countries had joined the European Union, making a total of twenty-five. The small country of Slovenia was one of those ten. In the little city of Goricia on the Italian-Slovenian border, preparations to dismantle the old Yugoslav border began. It touched our hearts to see that wall – about two feet high topped by barbed wire fencing – come down. That was the spot where Ivan and I had jumped across from Yugoslavia to Italy on June 22, 1957. The dismantling occurred just 54 days short of forty-seven years since we had crossed.

The European border would now be between Croatia and Slovenia. Newscasters explained that there would be five entrances, some from Slovenia and others from Hungary.

(Amanda and I on Kupa River on Jurovski Brod.)

One entrance is now in Zakanje County *(created from part of the original Ribnik County)*, across the Kupa River at the small Slovenian city of Metlika and the Croatian town of Jurovski Brod.

We rejoiced over Croatia's independence after nearly nine centuries of struggle, but we also were grateful for the opportunities we had found to see our dreams come true in our adopted country. America had given us everything we wished to have. We had no idea that we would be able to advance in our lives here without higher education and fluent English. But we found that in America, anything is possible. We are not rich but we never wanted to be – we wished only to have comfortable living conditions, which we have now.

We also fell in love with the American people. When we came here, they showed us kindness and understanding. Although we couldn't speak their language at first, they didn't make fun of us; instead, they said, "We understand everything you say to us." Although they knew we didn't have as much education as some of them did, they still treated us the same as if we were highly educated people. People would often remark, "You have lived in different countries; you know more than we do." They may have been exaggerating, but it made us feel good. Perhaps Americans are so understanding of foreign people because their own country became populated with immigrants like us from all over the world.

We have made many friends here, although the greatest of our love will always be for our children and grandchildren. Whatever Ivan and I accomplished in our lives we did for love of and hope for our future generations. Ivan often commented, "If I had thought we wouldn't have children, I would have spent every day whatever money I made." But God blessed us with two children, and we gave them the best lives we could.

Sometimes our family circle grew. A young girl from Zagreb, named Gordana Mandic, arrived in Kansas City to visit her sister, Ivana, and her family. Brian and Gordana were introduced by mutual friends, and he brought her to our

home for Ivan and me to meet her. Brian and Gordana were married in court on April 21, 2001, in order to speed up Gordana's immigration paper work; then they had a church wedding on November 3rd. And, so, our family became larger. *(Above: Brian and Gordana's wedding included Ivan, me, Simone and my father Janko.)*

In 2004, though, our Kansas City family got smaller. In July, Dean and Simone decided to move to Florida where they bought a condo. We knew we would miss them and Amanda, our first grandchild, although we tried to make things easier by pretending not to be sad. We wanted them to grow through their own life experiences, just as Ivan and I had. We were, however, happy later that same week when little Joshua was born on July 22, 2004, to Brian and Gordana.

A few years later, Dean would get a job in Washington, D.C., working for our government. After commuting back to Florida for two years, though, they decided to move permanently nearer to Dean's work. Amanda, twelve years old at the time, was excited to live close to American politics, something that interested her even at such a young age. She said, "No place in the world I'd rather be than where I live now." Good luck, Amanda!

(Simone and her family attend wedding in Canada of my brother Drago's granddaughter Natasha. Right, her groom gets in the picture, too.)

In 2005, Ivan and I were able to look back on our years together. January 8, 2005, marked our fiftieth wedding anniversary. We had gone through so much in those years, but we were proud of what we had been able to accomplish in the country we had chosen as our home.

On November 13, 2008, my father, John Bosiljevac, died at age ninety-five. He had lived longer than anyone else in my family. When I was young, I had admired his understanding of world affairs, and after he came to America he had been a great help to me with information for this book. After mother's death in 1995, father had moved next door to us, and for thirteen years I had visited him every evening. That was when I asked him to share with me his memories of our family and other members of our Croatian community.

A year after father's death, my brother Drago died in Croatia on December 17, 2009. *(Right: Drago's grandchildren, Heidi and Karlo Bosiljevac in Croatia.)*

Just after New Year, 2010, the winter brought us a lot of snow in Kansas City. Ivan, now almost eighty years old, continued to shovel our driveway despite my protests. He had been stubborn all of his life, and continued to be when he was old. A physical examination by his doctor on January 15th was called routine. On January 8th, Ivan and I went to a restaurant to celebrate our fifty-fifth anniversary.

Simone and Dean had asked us to visit them in Florida for Easter. Ivan didn't want to go but insisted that I go. Ivan promised he would go fishing with his friend Slavo Ivicak, whom I had asked to look out for Ivan. I called Ivan every evening and everything seemed normal, but on March 30th I couldn't reach him. I phoned Slavo, but couldn't get him either. When I called Brian and Gordana, five-year-old Joshua answered. "Joshua," I exclaimed, "where are dad and mom?" He explained, "Mom isn't home and dad is in the shower." Then he added, "But, grandma, today mom and I were at grandpa's house and he got dizzy. He fell in his chair."

My heart sank, "Joshua, tell dad to call me right after he gets out of the shower."

(Ivan's last joy with Joshua on his birthday.)

Gordana and Slavo had been with Ivan in the hospital, but my stubborn husband hadn't wanted them to call me. But of course I got the first flight I could and rushed to the hospital. Nurses said they thought he had had a stroke. He could understand and could hold his arms and legs up for a count of ten, but couldn't speak. What kind of stroke is that? I wondered, but had to wait till the next morning for the answer.

The doctor who arrived introduced himself as a cancer specialist. "Do you think my husband has cancer," I asked, and he said, "Yes." He asked me how much I wanted to know. "Everything," I replied. So he took me to his computer and showed me, starting with the lungs. One was full of cancer. His liver, then his brain, all showed the disease. Cancer has four stages, he told me, and Ivan is stage four. I realized there was no chance for his recovery. How could this be? His checkup had been clear. Just a few days earlier he had been eating, fishing, walking and speaking!

On April 10th Ivan was moved to a hospice where a nurse attended him constantly. We left late in the afternoon, but the nurse called us that evening. Ivan had died in room No. 7.

Although it may seem strange to others, two numbers have always been important in my life -- some for happy occasions, others sad: I had been born in House No. 7 in Brdo, and Ivan had died in room No. 7. My mother had been born in 1915 and I in 1935. Ivan and I married in 1955, and jumped the fence to freedom in 1957. Our daughter-in-law was born in 1975. My mother died in 1995; our granddaughter was born in 1995. My father died when he was 95 years old; Drago was 75 when he died. Ivan died when we had been married 55 years, in the year that I became 75.

Ivan and I had weathered many difficulties during our married life. We supported each other in everything, and whatever we accomplished we did together. Each of us had specific duties, but we always asked the other to approve any undertaking. My first responsibilities were children, home, bills, and savings. Any home repairs we did together. Ivan was always best at his job. When he worked for others, he didn't complain if company bosses asked him to work day and night. He learned his trade well, and when we had our own business, he took care of the shop and the employees, leaving the office completely to me. He would ask me to tell him how we stood financially, just signing necessary documents. We always faced life together. Those fifty-five years of sharing life with Ivan have given me many wonderful memories.

The year 2010 marked the beginning of a new stage in my life. My husband and parents were gone, Brian was running the family business, and Simone and her family were busy with their lives in the Washington, D.C. area. I longed to visit my brother Jure and his family and see my homeland at least one more time. When I called Simone and Dean to tell them, Dean was home alone. He asked, "Would you want to take your granddaughter with you?" Of course, if she wanted to go, I'd be delighted!

We flew to Zagreb's airport where Jure and his daughter Jadranka waited to greet us and take us first to Grice.

Nothing was as I had left it fifty-three years earlier, but at least the property on which I was born looked lovely, thanks to Jure and his wife Ana who continue to take care of our beautiful yard and of the gorgeous house which they built as a second home. I could not get enough of walking on that yard and looking at those fruit trees my brother had planted. They even have a paved street clear to their house, something we couldn't have dreamed of. Before his death Drago had renewed our old house. Now his son Kruno takes care of it, and he and his family use it on weekends. That original house, *at right in this photo*, looks wonderful, although it is 106 years old! *(The new one is at the left.)*

In spite of the improvements that our family and some others have been able to make, Grice is now just a pale shadow of the bright, warm remembered place it has in my heart. When I grew up there, every house contained family members, and neighbors shared the little they had when friends needed them. Places like the one where we lived offered few modern conveniences, but the air and the water were clean, and we ate natural food. We had no cancer, strokes or heart attacks because we ate vegetables, fruit and whole grain bread. Meat was available only on rare occasions. Having no cars, we walked everywhere, so despite hard work and not enough food, our bodies remained strong. For generation after generation, Ribnik County had been a lively place. We had traveled on foot to school *(See photo of school on facing page)*, church, a store, the post office, to visit relatives and to work in our fields.

(Lipnik School, attended by many of the Ribnik County children.)

During the communist era, most of us emigrated, and only a few older people live there now. Life became even harder for those who stayed. Most of those homes are sadly empty now, and few farms are being cultivated. Before Ivan and I left, we could see all of Grice from Brdo or Jarmek's Valley, but now there are trees on many farmlands so one can no longer walk on those fields that covered the hills and valleys. There are now no permanent residents in Brdo, although my family has kept up our property and uses it occasionally. Only a few people now live in three properties in all of Grice.

One change, however, was quite evident. That is in our cemetery by Libnik church, on the edge of Lipnik forest *(photo below.)* When I was young, only a few rich families had monuments on their plots. All others had only wooden crosses. Now I couldn't walk between the fancy, crowded monuments. All of those names I saw there I also see here in our Catholic cemetery in Kansas City, Kansas. Next to Libnik

church is the school my parents walked to, and I did as well for one year during the war when our teacher was gone.

When Amanda and I arrived at our property on Brdo, we found nearly all of the conveniences we had in America. This is a beautiful house with electricity, piped water, two showers, televisions and a telephone.

(Amanda at Jure's new house at Brdo.)

However, when night came, Amanda became frightened of the quiet there, so close to the forest. The next day I took her for a walk to Jarmek's Valley, to the house where Ivan and I had lived with his family. The house and outbuildings are still standing, although nobody lives there anymore. We took a few pictures and went on our way to see some of the neighbors. There I met a man about my age. We just stared for a while until I asked, "Who are you?" "Janko Jarmek," he replied, and I smiled. "I am Ana Jarmek." We shook hands, laughing because we hadn't recognized each other after fifty-three years. We walked to another neighbor's. I didn't recognize him, either. It was Jure Jarmek. I had no idea his brother Miho and wife Katarina were visiting from Venezuela. I hadn't seen Miho since 1957 when he, Ivan and I were together in Italy.

Going to another property which Ivan's family owned, we heard loud music at a neighbor's house in which nobody lives. Amanda spotted a van from Canada there, so I knocked on the door and called out, "Is anybody there?" No one answered. I told Amanda that Jure Horvat, our old neighbor who died, had a daughter in Canada. We heard later from others that it was the daughter's son, Marin Janakovic, who had been there. We discovered that we couldn't even come close to see the house that Ivan's family had owned because it was completely surrounded with trees and brush, so we turned for home.

(Ivan's niece, Ljubica, and her family in Canada)

Amanda and I walked through the forest on our way back. Amanda was very excited, but I was a little frightened, fearing there might be a wolf or a bear in that place that had been a clear area when I lived there. Growing up, little could frighten me, but when we came back to my brother's house I was relieved that we were safely out of that jungle-like forest.

On another day we went to see a lady who was my friend during our teenage years. I found her and another lady sitting on a roadside bench between

Jarmek's Valley and Fabac Little Mountain.

Ljuba (Fabac) Zeljeznjak and Ljuba Secan didn't recognize me, nor I them, but soon we remembered our youth. My friend asked if I remembered taking a picture of us and Dragica (Jarmek) Jarnevic during  Saint Ana's Festival. I told her I still had the picture. I had seen Dragica in 1992, but she had since died. *(Ljuba Fabac, Ana Bosiljevac, Draga Jarmek in our church clothes at St. Ana's festival.)*

My brother Jure, his friend, Mirko Hadusek, and I did take another picture as a reminder of the time we went to get apples and Drago Zeleznjak chased us; but my childhood friend, Drago Bosiljevac, who had shared in that adventure, lives now in Pittsburg, Pennsylvania, with his family.

My biggest surprise came when we met seven young people. We found out that they had never lived there, but all of them were grandchildren of former residents: Marin Janakovic from Canada, Jure Jarmek's two granddaughters from Karlovac, Janko Jarmek's son, and three grandsons of Ivan's brother, who are living in Lipnik. My granddaughter Amanda made eight. Surprisingly, all of them speak English. I was really touched to see those young people – our descendants – talking and laughing together. I said, "When I was as young as you are now, your grandfathers and grandmothers and I would meet here and talk, just as you are doing now. Since we scattered to other cities and continents, we could never have imagined that our grandchildren would meet here and speak English!" It was a defining moment for me. The wonderful circle of life in Grice remained unbroken.

Before we headed for home, Jure and Ana took us to Zagreb, Croatia's capital city.

Amanda was fascinated by the sarcophagus of Kardinal Alojzije Stepinac displayed in Zagreb's cathedral,

and the architect-ural details of Saint Mark's Church by the Croatian parli-ament.

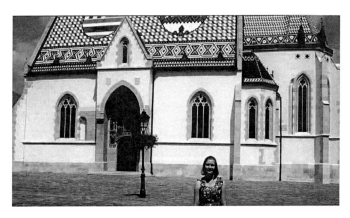

Another day we visited Plitvice, Croatia's most spectacular waterfall, then on to Bled, the famous lake of Slovenia. We stayed a few days in my brother's apartment at Novi Grad, sightseeing at Porec and Rovinj on the Adriatic coast. Then it was time to leave, as Amanda needed to start school in America.

It had given me great pleasure to take young Amanda on this trip, sharing with her the sights and memories of that beautiful area of Croatia in which I had grown up. I hope that she – and perhaps those who read this memoir – will understand and appreciate the life experiences, some enjoyable and some sad, as well as the traditions that were ours many years ago.

Author's Note

Since the numbers 7 and 5 have always been involved in my life experiences, it seems appropriate to end this Memoir here with my 75th birthday on November 19th, 2010.

Ana Bosiljevac Jarmek

Appendix: Surnames of Lipnik County

Baic
Barbic
Barbiric
Basarac
Baska
Belanic
Bert
Blazevic
Bosiljevac
Bradica
Bravaric
Brinc
Broz
Brozinic
Bucan
Budacki
Buncic
Buric
Car
Cigic
Colner
Crnic
Cavlovic
Cavlovicak
Dehlic
Dolinar
Dragos
Draskovic
Drgastin
Dukovcic
Dupin
Erdeljac
Fabac
Fabac-Ivesko
Fabac-Lugar
Fabac-Misko
Fabina
Filipas
Fracul
Frankovic
Furlic
Gebic
Gojmerac
Golubic
Gorican
Gorup
Grasa
Grdinovac
Grguric
Hadusek
Hajsan

Horvat
Horvatin
Jacmenovic
Jadric
Jagas
Jaklevic
Jaksa
Jambrosic
Jarmek
Jarnevic
Jarsulic
Juranic
Kezele
Kladusan
Klemencic
Klobucar
Kohanic
Komidar
Kralj
Kralj-Novosel
Krasevac
Krstulic
Krznaric
Krznaric-Grasa
Kuzmic
Ladesic
Likovic
Lukac
Macan
Makar
Malinaric
Mance
Matan
Mihelic
Mikoni
Miljavac
Milkovic
Modrcin
Moravac
Mravunac
Muc
Muhic
Munjak
Mus
Novosel
Ofak
Pavic
Pazderac
Persin
Pestak
Petrusic

Pihner
Piskuric
Plavan
Pozeg
Pozeg-Vancas
Radman
Radman-Belanic
Ratkaj
Resovac
Ropar
Rozgaj
Rozman
Sambol
Samovojska
Secen
Secen-Jurcev
Secen-Matuljak
Skratski
Slak
Sopcic
Spoja
Spudic
Srakovcic
Srbelj
Srbelj-Dehlic
Staresina
Staresinic
Stipan
Stojkovic
Suljada
Simec
Skvorac
Sporcic
Stajcer
Straus
Suljak
Tomasic
Tomecalj
Trzok
Vajda
Vancas
Vardijan
Veselic
Vivodinac
Vrabac
Wiedervol
Zmajic
Zeljeznjak
Zugecic
Zgelj
Zupetic

Other Family Memorabilia

Left:
Ivan and I dance following Brian and Gordana's wedding in 2001.

Below:
In 2010, Amanda stands on the porch of the house Ivan was born in. It had been remodeled.

Above Left to right: I with granddaughter Amanda and daughter Simone in front of the White House in 2010. Amanda thinks this is the best place in the world!

Right: Dean and Simone's engagement picture.

Above: My son Brian and wife Gordana, and grandson Joshua . . .
with a sad face.

Right:

Same grandson, Joshua; same shirt as above, but with his usual happy face.

Amanda
juggles
apples
in front of
Jure's
house
. . .

as I, with Jure and Mirko Hadusek reminisce about our
childhood years in Brdo . . .

and Jure's grandson Mark
shows that he has inherited
his grandpa's business
abilities.